Instant Library Lessons

Second Grade

Karen A. Farmer Wanamaker

UpstartBooks

Fort Atkinson, Wisconsin

To Mom and Pop
for their lifelong commitment to learning and libraries.

Published by UpstartBooks
W5527 State Road 106
P.O. Box 800
Fort Atkinson, Wisconsin 53538-0800
1-800-448-4887

© Karen A. Farmer Wanamaker, 2005
Cover design and illustrations by Debra Neu

The paper used in this publication meets the minimum requirements of
American National Standard for Information Sciences —
Permanence of Paper for Printed Library Materials. ANSI/NISO Z39.48-1992.

Dewey, DDC and Dewey Decimal Classification are registered trademarks of OCLC Online Computer
Library Center, Incorporated.

Contents

 Introduction

When I was in college preparing to become a Library Media Specialist, I had no idea how important my experiences with and love for designing curriculum would become. Once I reached the real world I quickly realized that everyone in an elementary school had textbooks, workbooks, teachers' editions, or at the very least, a list of objectives—everyone, that is, except the Library Media Specialist.

Through the years I searched for a source of lesson plans that provided for the needs of Library Media Specialists and their students. In the meantime I created my own lessons. This was actually a plus as I truly enjoyed the creative process. Unfortunately, there was never enough time to fully develop the lesson ideas with all that had to be done in the library. Now I have the opportunity to do what I always thought someone ought to do. This book is designed to provide a year's worth of lessons—all that is needed are the suggested books and the children.

These lessons were specifically designed to support the following educational beliefs:

- Instruction should include exposure to fiction and nonfiction at all levels.

- Learning experiences are most successful when taught in a consistent frame that moves learning from whole class instruction through teamwork and working in pairs before expecting children to work alone.

- In order for students to have the best opportunity to learn, adults should foster higher levels of thinking by asking questions that encourage thought and by teaching students to ask their own thought-provoking questions.

- Using children's literature to direct learning is most appropriate when addressing library instruction.

- Interactive instruction based on what is known about learning styles provides the best environment for learning.

- Library instruction should fully support the school-wide curriculum.

How to Use This Book

The length and number of library sessions varies greatly from library to library, and often from school year to school year within the same location. Many other factors, such as the number of students per class and the amount of checkout time needed, contribute to the amount of instructional time available in a library.

For these reasons, this book was designed to provide 36 one-hour lessons. Each lesson can be used in one session or broken into smaller segments for multiple sessions. These lessons offer Library Media Specialists choices in determining the makeup of their particular library class instruction.

The Instant Library Lessons series includes Lesson Learning Ideas that encompass the following instructional strands:

- **Library Skills:** Including, but not limited to, research and learning skills.

- **Literature Appreciation:** Exposure to and experience with a variety of print genres.

- **Techniques of Learning:** Strategies such as questioning skills and interactive learning that support lifelong learning.

- **Comprehension:** Developing learning processes that support effective readers and learners.

- **Writing Experiences:** Fostering the link between reading and writing needed throughout a lifetime.

- **Oral Language:** Opportunities to develop and refine skills in interpersonal communication from speaking, listening and viewing.

Each individual lesson includes:

- **Featured Book(s).** The book or books the lesson is based upon with corresponding summary information.

- **Lesson Learning Ideas.** Specific lesson objectives based on the instructional strands developed for Instant Library Lessons. See pages 12–14.

- **Materials.** Items to be collected prior to instruction. Ordering information is available (see pages 187–189 for details) so the needed items can be obtained as easily as possible.

- **Before Class.** A list of tasks to complete before teaching the lesson.

- **Lesson Plan.** Presented in a format that can be followed step by step or altered to meet your specific needs.

Suggested Library Set-Up

In order to fully implement all of the lesson ideas included in this book a sample room layout has been created (see page 11). Recommendations include:

- Library furniture that includes enough tables and chairs to accommodate all of the students from one class within a given area. Each table should have a permanent container (basket) with crayons or markers, scissors and glue. Additional items, such as books or lesson materials, can be added when necessary. A permanent table sign label will assist in giving directions to students.

- A gathering area that provides for a more intimate sharing of books and learning experiences. The gathering area will need a stool or chair for the librarian. The students can sit on the floor. A big book stand, overhead projector on a movable cart, screen, easel with chart paper or chalkboard, TV with VCR and/or DVD complete the needed equipment.

- Other items which help organize the library setting might include: a movable book return cart located near the library entrance; a movable cart or table for a container of shelf markers and to display check-out name cards in divided containers; and a place for free reading materials (this could be a section within existing book shelves and/or a table space and should have enough room to accommodate a laundry-sized basket and several smaller baskets).

Tips of the Trade

- **Ready Rhyme.** Whenever students are seated on the floor, teach them this rhyme to help them learn how to get ready to listen. You can use the sign language words provided to go with the rhyme. Repeat the rhyme with motions until all of the students are ready.

  If you are seated on your bottom, *(Sit)*
  With your legs crossed,
  And your eyes this way, *(Look)*
  You're ready, *(Ready)*
  You're ready,
  You're ready,
  Yea.

| **Sit** | **Look** | **Ready** |

- When you need to get your children's attention, teach them these words in sign language:

Stop   **Look**   **Listen**

Do not continue until every student is participating in the signing.

- When it is time for students to line up to leave the library call one table at a time. This can be done by labeling each table with a different color table sign. Then use sign language or a foreign language to instruct the students when it is their turn. For example, say and/or sign the following phrase:

Red Table, line up slowly and quietly.

Then, continue with yellow, green, blue, black, white, purple, orange or whatever colors you choose. Use one of the following Web sites to locate sign language information: *www.handspeak.com* or *www.mastertech-home.com/ASLDict.html.*

- In order to get a line of children all going in the same direction teach them to "ENT." (If your eyes, ears, nose and throat are facing the door you are ready to go!)

- **Wiggle Squeezers.** Often during instruction students will need to take a break. Use one or more of the following movement activities to provide a break.

Shake Your Sillies Out

<u>Verse 1</u>: *(Hold hands slightly above waist level with elbows bent at 90 degree angle. Rotate arms and hips from side to side in a twisting motion. On the last line of the verse, point index fingers while moving hands up and down at the wrist.)*
You've got to shake, shake, shake your sillies out.
Shake, shake, shake your sillies out.
Shake, shake, shake your sillies out.
And wiggle your waggles away.

<u>Verse 2</u>: Clap your crazies out. *(Clap hands on first three lines. On the last line of the verse, point index fingers while moving hands up and down at the wrist.)*

<u>Verse 3</u>: Stretch your stretchies out. *(Stretch arms in various directions on the first three lines. On the last line of the verse, point index fingers while moving hands up and down at the wrist.)*

<u>Verse 4</u>: Jump your jingles out. *(Jump up and down in place on the first three lines of the rhyme. On the last line of the verse, point index fingers while moving hands up and down at the wrist.)*

<u>Verse 5</u>: Yawn your yuckies out. *(Slow down the pace of the chant and speak softly during this verse. On the first three lines cover your mouth and yawn while inhaling during the word "yawn." On the last line of the verse, point index fingers while moving hands up and down at the wrist.)*

Hi, My Name is Joe

Hi, my name is Joe.
I've got a wife and three kids,
And I work in a button factory.
One day the boss came in,
He said, "Joe, are you busy?"
I said, "No."
He said, "Do it like this."

The first time just say the words. Then add a motion and repeat the words again while doing the motion. At the end of each verse, add an additional movement while continuing each of the previous movements.

Suggested movements: *Wave right hand; wave left hand; raise and lower one foot; march in place by raising and lowering each foot one at a time; and nod head. On the last verse change the words to: Joe, are you busy? I said, yes!*

Oliver Twist

Oliver, twist, twist, twist,
(Place your hands on your hips and twist side to side each time you say "twist.")
Can't do this, this, this, *(Stretch both arms high over head.)*
Touch your toes, toes, toes, *(Bend at the waist and touch your fingers to your toes.)*
Nobody nose, nose, nose.
(Place your right hand into your left palm and touch your nose with both hands.)

Say the rhyme three times, repeating it faster each time. Then do the rhyme one last time in extra slow motion to calm the children down.

Do Your Ears Hang Low?

Do your ears hang low? *(Backs of hands on ears, fingers down.)*
Do they wobble to and fro? *(Sway fingers.)*
Can you tie 'em in a knot? *(Tie large knot in air.)*
Can you tie 'em in a bow? *(Draw bow in air with both hands.)*
Can you throw 'em over your shoulder, *(Throw both hands over left shoulder.)*
Like a continental soldier? *(Salute.)*
Do your ears hang low? *(Backs of hands on ears, fingers down.)*

Always do the last verse in extra slow motion to calm the children down and prepare them to return to work.

- **Free Reading Area.** Throughout the lessons there are suggested materials for the "Free Reading Area." Note the map under suggested library set-up to see where to locate such materials. These are self-directed materials students can use when they have wait time. Wait time most often occurs during check out since all children can't select a book at the same time. Establish guidelines for using the materials within your library. Be sure to introduce and practice how to use the materials before they appear in the Free Reading Area.

Materials for a free reading area might include:

- Velcro boards, aprons and mitts with story pieces in plastic bags based on Literature Pictures

- metal boards with story pieces in plastic bags based on Literature Pictures

- minute books—brief, paperback books for early readers

- children's magazines

Add items as recommended in the lesson plans. Rotate items so students don't get bored with the offerings. House similar items in plastic baskets for easy access and clean up.

Literature Pictures (LPs)

Literature Pictures work well for presentations and Free Reading Area materials.

1. Make copies of the pictures.

2. Color the pictures. If coloring anything the size of your hand or smaller, it should be colored with the thick lead, colored art pencils. These can be found in art stores (Hobby Lobby or Michael's) or some school supply stores and catalogs. The brand that has been most successful is Prismacolor. If enlarging the pictures so they are larger than your hand, artist pastel chalks work well. After coloring, lightly spray the pictures with cheap hairspray. Most of the pastels found in school and art supply stores are fine for this activity.

3. Back each piece with poster board. Use spray glue, which is often called spray adhesive. This makes for a smooth finish and can be bought at paint and discount stores. Cut out the pieces.

4. Write any cues needed for telling the story on the back of the individual pieces. Then laminate and cut out the pieces.

5. Decide between making the story into a Velcro apron story or a metal board presentation. For an apron version, back the pieces with adhesive-backed Velcro but also glue them with Tacky glue. For a metal board story, use the adhesive-backed magnetic strips and Tacky glue.

Library Table Signs

1. Decide how to identify tables (by colors, numbers, letters or pictures). Instant Library Lessons uses colors.

2. Buy free-standing plastic picture frames (available in 8" x 10" or 5" x 7" from discount stores) for each table.

3. Create a different table identifier for each table in the appropriate size and place it in a frame.

4. Place a sign in the middle of each student table.

Great Rip Roar Read Report

1. Make copies of the Great Rip Roar Read Report on page 150.

2. Train the students to look for damage before leaving the library with a book.

3. If a student finds a book that needs repair he or she should fill out the report, then place the report in the damaged book and put them in the designated location.

Sample Room Layout

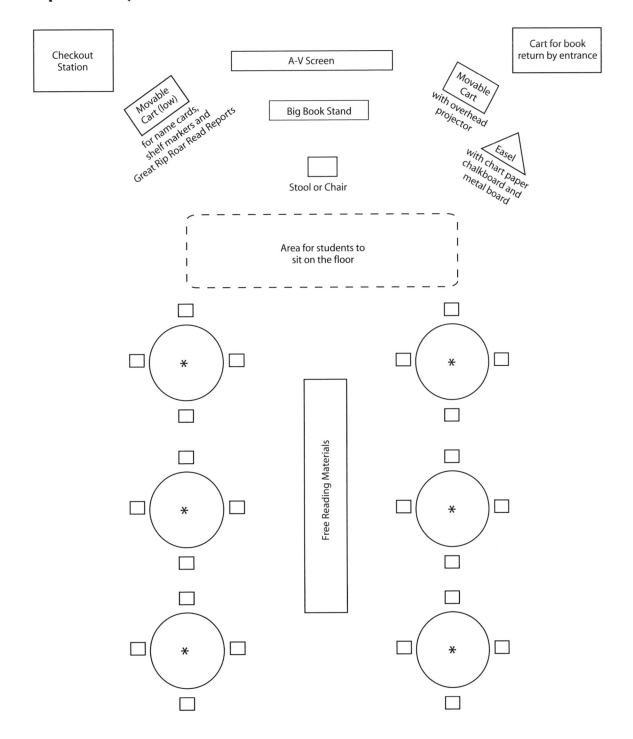

* table signs, baskets with colors, scissors, pencils and glue

One or more of the movable carts and/or big book stand should include storage for lesson materials for current lessons and lesson plan book.

❁ Lesson Learning Ideas ❁

The lesson learning ideas encompass six instructional strands. See page 6 for an explanation of each strand.

Library Skills

• Knows that materials in the library have a specific location and order

• Can identify the spine and spine label of a book

• Can locate a book in the easy fiction section by the author's last name

• Knows the spine label tells where a book is placed on the shelf

• Uses multiple resources to locate information

• Is developing a basic concept of the research process

• Can locate and identify the basic parts of a book

• Is familiar with basic reference books and their purpose

• Is familiar with the Dewey Decimal Classification® system

• Is able to identify, utilize and create basic parts of a book

• Can read and comprehend call number information

• Can utilize alphabetical order as needed for location purposes

Literature Appreciation

• Has had experience with various literary genres

• Has used fiction and nonfiction materials

• Has an understanding of the concept of artist and illustrator

• Has an initial understanding of the difference between fiction and nonfiction

• Knows the meaning of award-winning literature

• Has an understanding of how authors write books

• Understands and applies nonfiction reading techniques

• Understands and applies the concepts of fiction and nonfiction

• Has experience with literary based drama

• Understands the concept of book series and how they are linked by common characters

Techniques of Learning

- Has established visual literacy skills
- Has experience in critical thinking questioning
- Has the opportunity to work in cooperative groups
- Has experience with compare and contrast questioning
- Understands and participates in brainstorming activities
- Is able to integrate cues from written and visual text
- Uses organizational formats for learning
- Can transfer learning experiences across multiple situations
- Attends to personal and/or team tasks outside of the whole group setting
- Takes an active role in recomposing visual and written information
- Can appropriately access, evaluate and apply Internet-sourced information

Comprehension

- Has extended personal vocabulary
- Has experience in the comprehension strategy of retelling
- Has the opportunity to apply the comprehension strategy of story structure
- Has the opportunity to participate in experiences that support the acquisition of fluency
- Utilizes the comprehension strategy of prediction
- Is able to set a purpose for reading
- Is able to make connections with prior knowledge and experience
- Can recall, summarize and paraphrase what is listened to and viewed
- Is beginning to comprehend basic text structures
- Is developing the ability to generate appropriate questions
- Has experience with reading for the purpose of extending knowledge and understanding
- Applies the skill of sequencing as an organizational strategy for comprehension

Writing Experiences

- Has participated in a variety of age-appropriate writing experiences
- Can create labels, notes and/or captions
- Is able to generate brief descriptions that use sensory details

- Responds to literature in a variety of written formats
- Uses prewriting strategies such as drawings, brainstorming and/or graphic organizers
- Imitates models of good writing
- Is able to transfer ideas into sentences with appropriate support
- Indicates an understanding of story structure necessary for narrative writing
- Participates in narrative writing experiences
- Participates in descriptive writing experiences
- Participates in expository writing experiences
- Participates in persuasive writing experiences
- Has experience with examples of narrative writing and its uses
- Has experience with examples of descriptive writing and its uses
- Has experience with examples of expository writing and its uses
- Has experience with examples of persuasive writing and its uses

Oral Language

- Has taken part in storytelling and read aloud experiences
- Participates in audience participation storytelling
- Is able to listen to and comprehend a variety of oral presentation formats
- Is able to listen to and comprehend a variety of multimedia presentation formats
- Is developing the ability to respond to what is seen and heard
- Has participated in oral presentation experiences

Out of this World

Out of this World · Lesson 1

Featured Book

Alistair in Outer Space by Marilyn Sadler. Simon & Schuster, 1988.

When Alistair is kidnapped by a spaceship full of Goots from Gootula, his main concern is for his overdue library books. ISBN 0671666789

Lesson Learning Ideas

Literature Appreciation

- Understands and applies the concepts of fiction and nonfiction

- Has had experience with various literary genres

Techniques of Learning

- Has experience with compare and contrast questioning

- Has experience in critical thinking questioning

Comprehension

- Utilizes the comprehension strategy of prediction

Materials

- *Alistair in Outer Space* by Marilyn Sadler

- *Alistair in Outer Space* Reading Rainbow video (see Ordering Information, page 151)

- True vs. Make-believe Chart with Alistair and the Goot (page 18)

- Alistair Reminder Note (page 19)

Before Class

1. Number the pages in *Alistair in Outer Space* starting with the first page of text.

2. Set the video to start with the picture of LeVar Burton in Washington, D.C.

3. Make copies of the True vs. Make-believe Chart.

4. Fill in the day and make a copy of the Alistair Reminder Note for each child.

Lesson Plan

1. Read the title and show the cover of *Alistair in Outer Space*. Ask the students what "outer space" is, where it is and how you know when you are there. Record the ideas the students provide, remembering to prompt students to include what they are basing their ideas upon. (Save this information for a later lesson.)

2. Show the seven-minute Reading Rainbow video segment of *Alistair in Outer Space*. End the viewing segment with the end of the book.

3. Discuss the idea of fiction and nonfiction. Have the children decide what section of the library today's story would fit. Remind them how they are asked to provide proof when they express ideas in library discussions.

4. Have the students work as a class or in pairs to look at the pictures from the book and decide which ones show something that could be real (picture of Alistair) and which ones show things that are not real (picture of a Goot). Make a chart of the pictures that fit into each category. Provide a few examples to get the students started. **Note:** Some of the pages could go in either or both categories.

   • Looking at page 2, could there be a real boy named Alistair? *Yes*

   • Looking at pages 11–12, are there Goots who live in outer space? *No*

True	Make-believe
Page 2	Pages 7–8
Page 3	Pages 11–12
Page 4	Page 14
Page 5	Pages 15–16
Page 6	Page 17
Pages 9–10	Page 18
Page 13	Pages 19-20
Page 26	Pages 21–22
Page 34	Pages 23–24
Pages 35–36	Page 25
	Page 27
	Page 28
	Page 29
	Page 30
	Pages 31–32
	Page 33

5. Discuss how the chart proves that the book is a work of fiction.

6. Introduce science fiction as a special kind of fiction that takes scientific facts, like space travel by humans, and asks "What if?" by mixing in make-believe elements. In this story the author might be asking:

   - What if there really were other beings in outer space?

   - What if space creatures came to Earth and took a human?

7. Direct the students' attention to the end of the story. The book ends with Alistair landing in Antarctica, which the sign (in the video) says is 9,000 miles from the library. Have the students develop answers to "What if they ended up in Antarctica? How would they get home and how long would it take?"

8. Give each child an Alistair Reminder Note below to help them remember when to return their library books.

Remember...

My library books are due on:

 # Out of this World · Lesson 2

Featured Books

From Here to There by Margery Cuyler. Henry Holt & Company, 1999.

Maria introduces herself as a member of a specific family and as having a definite address and place in the universe. ISBN 080503191X

Me and My Place in Space by Joan Sweeney. Bantam Doubleday Dell, 1999.

A child describes how the earth, sun and planets are part of our solar system, which is just a small part of the universe. ISBN 0517885905

My Place in Space by Robin and Sally Hirst. Scholastic, 1992.

Henry tells the bus driver exactly where he lives, positioning himself precisely in the universe. ISBN 0531070301

Lesson Learning Ideas

Literature Appreciation

- Has used fiction and nonfiction materials

Techniques of Learning

- Can transfer learning experiences across multiple situations

Comprehension

- Has extended personal vocabulary

Writing Experiences

- Has participated in a variety of age-appropriate writing experiences

- Responds to literature in a variety of written formats

Oral Language

- Is developing the ability to respond to what is seen and heard

Materials

- *From Here to There* by Margery Cuyler

- *Me and My Place in Space* by Joan Sweeney

- *My Place in Space* by Robin and Sally Hirst

- notebook paper, pencils and crayons
- address chart visual (page 22)
- map of the world

Before Class

Prepare the address chart visual so that it can be used for whole class instruction.

Lesson Plan

1. Give the students paper and ask them to write down their addresses. Ask several students to share their addresses with the class. Discuss why we have addresses and why students need to know their address. Remind students that they learned their address by the time they were in kindergarten. Today they are going to learn another way of expressing their addresses.

2. Read *My Place in Space* aloud.

3. Five of the last six pages in the story show the address for the characters. Share the chart. Ask students how much of this address would be the same as their own addresses. Locate Australia on a map. Walk through country and hemisphere information for the characters in the book and the students.

4. Read *From Here to There* aloud. Create an address chart for the character in the book (person's name, family members, street address, town, county, state, country, continent, hemisphere, planet, solar system, galaxy, universe).

5. Compare the two sets of addresses from the books shared in the lesson. Have the students combine the two addresses into one complete address. Discuss how the children's addresses would fit into this format.

6. Give each student paper to write their own complete address and suggest that they may want to draw pictures to create their own address book.

7. If time permits, read aloud *Me and My Place in Space.* This is a different version of the address book that the students experienced in this lesson.

My Place in Space

Henry and Rosie Wilson

12 Main Street

Gumbridge, Australia

Southern Hemisphere

Planet Earth

Solar System

Solar Neighborhood

Orion Arm

Milky Way Galaxy

Local Group of Galaxies

Virgo Super Cluster

The Universe

Out of this World · Lesson 3

Lesson Learning Ideas

Library Skills

- Can identify the spine and spine label of a book

- Knows the spine label tells where a book is placed on the shelf

- Can read and comprehend call number information

Literature Appreciation

- Understands and applies the concepts of fiction and nonfiction

Writing Experiences

- Responds to literature in a variety of written formats

Materials

- books on space from the nonfiction section

- *Alistair in Outer Space* by Marilyn Sadler

- *From Here to There* by Margery Cuyler

- *Me and My Place in Space* by Joan Sweeney

- *My Place in Space* by Robin and Sally Hirst

- Book Address Frame (page 25)

Before Class

1. Gather the books needed for the lesson.

2. Make copies of the Book Address Frame for use by the class and individual students.

Lesson Plan

1. Show students numerous examples of traditional nonfiction books about space (Seymour Simon's books are good examples). Share pictures and text from some of the books. Ask the students what kinds of books these are. Explain that it used to be easy to tell nonfiction books from fiction books because nonfiction books contained only factual information and were usually written for students in fourth grade or older. That changed in 1986 when Joanna Cole wrote the first Magic School Bus book.

2. Bring back the four books already covered in this unit. Remind students that the books from the last lesson shared addresses for people. Tell them that today they are going to look at the addresses for books in a library. Show the spine label of each of the four books used previously in the unit. Two of the books are considered fiction and two are considered nonfiction. See if the children can decide which books are which by looking at the information on the spine label and the cover.

3. Explain to the students that the information on a spine label is the address of a book, or where it belongs on the shelf in a library. Demonstrate how the information is indicated in your library, such as E for Easy Fiction, etc.

4. As a class, use *Alistair in Outer Space* and create a book address for this book like the frame in *From Here to There*. Looking at another fiction book, discuss why *From Here to There* might be called a fiction book. Remind students it's not always easy to decide. Talk through the book address for this book.

5. Look at the spine labels for the two nonfiction books: *Me and My Place in Space* and *My Place in Space*. Explain that all of the information on a spine label, whether it is letters or numbers, is called a call number.

6. Share the differences for a book address for one of the nonfiction books. Explain that the students will learn more about the full meaning of the numbers in a later lesson. If time permits, let the students create a book address for the other nonfiction book.

Book Address Frame

My name or title is _____.

My writer or author is _____.

I live in the _____ section

of the _____ library.

I belong on the shelf in the _____

section with all of the other books written by authors whose last

names start with the letter _____ like

_____.

Out of this World · Lesson 4

Featured Book

The Magic School Bus Lost in the Solar System by Joanna Cole. Scholastic, 1990.

On a special field trip in the magic school bus, Ms. Frizzle's class goes into outer space and visits each planet in the solar system. ISBN 0590414283

Lesson Learning Ideas

Library Skills

- Can locate and identify the basic parts of a book

- Is able to identify, utilize and create basic parts of a book

Literature Appreciation

- Has used fiction and nonfiction materials

- Has an initial understanding of the difference between fiction and nonfiction

Oral Language

- Is able to listen to and comprehend a variety of multimedia presentation formats

Materials

- *The Magic School Bus at the Waterworks* by Joanna Cole

- *The Magic School Bus Lost in the Solar System* by Joanna Cole

- *The Magic School Bus Gets Lost in Space* video (see Ordering Information, page 151)

- all of the available books from the Magic School Bus series

- Magic School Bus stamp (see Ordering Information, page 151)

- construction paper

Before Class

1. Set the video to begin with the beginning of the story.

2. Gather all of the Magic School Bus books in your collection.

3. Create Magic School Bus bookmarks by cutting construction paper into strips and stamping each with the Magic School Bus stamp.

Lesson Plan

1. In the last lesson students were told that in 1986 the Magic School Bus series changed nonfiction writing completely. This happened because Joanna Cole's Magic School Bus series combined funny fiction with factual information that got students excited about reading nonfiction. In fact, her books are actually three books in one (see page 35 for an explanation).

2. Provide students with all of the Magic School Bus books in your library collection. Distribute the books among the students.

3. Review the concept of a title page. Have the students turn their Magic School Bus books to the first page with writing on it. Ask them to speculate on what this page is called. Remind students that a title page is found in the front of almost all books and it usually has no more than four pieces of information on it.

4. Have the students use the title page from a Magic School Bus book to decide what the four pieces of information might be (title, author, publisher and sometimes illustrator). Have the students find the author's name for their book. Explain that Joanna Cole did not write all of the books. She wrote the first books and created the format. Discuss what a publisher does for a book.

5. Have the students turn to the back of the title page. This page is called the verso of the title page. Among other things, this page includes the cataloging in publication information. Direct the students' attention to the Library of Congress Cataloging-in-Publication data. Remind the children that LeVar Burton was at the Library of Congress to introduce *Alistair in Outer Space.* Explain the summary, subject headings and date of publication.

6. Ask the students to locate the Magic School Bus book that was published in 1986. *(The Magic School Bus at the Waterworks)*

7. Show the beginning of the video *The Magic School Bus Gets Lost in Space.* Show the first 13 minutes of the story. Stop when the students lose Ms. Frizzle in the asteroid belt.

8. Give each student a bookmark as he or she leaves the library.

Out of this World · Lesson 5

Featured Books

Draw 50 Aliens, UFOs, Galaxy Ghouls, Milkyway Marauders, and other Extraterrestrial Creatures
by Lee Ames. Broadway Books, 1998.

A step-by-step guide to drawing outer space creatures. ISBN 038549145X

Ellen Ochoa **by Pam Walker. Scholastic Library Publishing, 2001.**

A short biography of astronaut Ellen Ochoa who is a Hispanic American. ISBN 0516234331

Exploring Space **by Robin Birch. Chelsea House, 2003.**

Describes the history of space exploration and what life is like for astronauts in a weightless environment. ISBN 0791069745

Galactic Giggles: Far-out and Funny Jokes about Outer Space
by Michael Dahl. Picture Window Books, 2003.

An easy-to-read collection of riddles about astronauts, stars and other objects in space. ISBN 140480126X

Our Solar System **by Seymour Simon. William Morrow & Co., 1992.**

Describes the origins and characteristics of the sun, moons, planets, asteroids, meteorites and comets. ISBN 0688099920

Space Travel **by Jenny Tesar. Heinemann Library, 1997.**

Provides an introduction to space travel, describing what astronauts do, how they live and work in space, space shuttles and space stations, moon landings and more. ISBN 1575725819

Lesson Learning Ideas

Library Skills

- Is familiar with the Dewey decimal classification system

- Can locate a book in the easy fiction section by the author's last name

- Knows the spine label tells where a book is placed on the shelf

- Can read and comprehend call number information

- Is familiar with basic reference books and their purpose

- Knows that materials in the library have a specific location and order

Literature Appreciation

- Has had experience with various literary genres

Materials

- *Draw 50 Aliens, UFOs, Galaxy Ghouls, Milkyway Marauders, and other Extraterrestrial Creatures* by Lee Ames
- *Ellen Ochoa* by Pam Walker
- *Exploring Space* by Robin Birch
- *Galactic Giggles: Far-out and Funny Jokes about Outer Space* by Michael Dahl
- *Our Solar System* by Seymour Simon
- *Rabbit and the Moon* by Douglas Wood
- *Space Travel* by Jenny Tesar
- The *Visual Dictionary of the Universe* by Sue Becklake
- Dewey Chart (page 31)
- art paper and crayons

Before Class

1. Gather the books in the materials list. If these are not available try to find a book about space from each of the following sections: 300, 500, 600, 700, 800, 900, biography and reference.

2. Reproduce the Dewey Chart so that the whole class can see it.

Lesson Plan

1. Remind students that books shelved in the fiction section are placed on the shelf by the author's last name. This is also done in nonfiction, but books are first put together in groups so that all of the books on a certain topic can be found together. Ask students to speculate why nonfiction books are organized this way.

2. Hand out all of the books for this lesson. Pretend that all of the librarians in the world are lost in space with Ms. Frizzle. It is up to the class to figure out where these books about space belong in the library.

3. Share the Dewey Chart. Do not draw attention to the call numbers yet. Explain that the classes in the nonfiction section are much like the classes of students in a school. For example, all of the students in _____ class are second graders. Do not focus on the names of the classes as much as the types of books found in each.

4. Have the students decide if any of the books they're looking at fit into each class as it is discussed. The summaries about the books may prove helpful.

5. After the activity show the children how to check the call number information on the book spine to see if they were correct.

   - *Visual Dictionary of the Universe* (reference)

   - *Rabbit and the Moon* by Douglas Wood (300)

   - *Our Solar System* by Seymour Simon (500)

   - *Space Travel* by Jenny Tesar (600)

   - *Draw 50 Aliens, UFOs, Galaxy Ghouls, Milkyway Marauders, and other Extraterrestrial Creatures* by Lee Ames (700)

   - *Galactic Giggles: Far-out and Funny Jokes about Outer Space* by Michael Dahl (800)

   - *Exploring Space* by Robin Birch (900)

   - *Ellen Ochoa* by Pam Walker (biography)

   The reference book can fit into the General Works or the Reference section in any particular library, whereas the book about Ellen Ochoa could be classified in the 600s or in the biography section. Make sure the students understand where to find these books in the library they are using.

6. Have the students locate the classes that did not have a space book (100, 200 and 400). Review the kinds of books found in these classes. Help the students make up space book titles for each class. Divide the ideas among the students and have them create a book cover and spine for each book. Ideas to get you started:

   - 100—Aliens or "true" stories like the Alistair story

   - 200—Planet names come from the names of Greek and Roman mythology

   - 400—If someday a speaking life form is found on another planet, there could be a book about their language

Dewey Chart

Class Numbers	Class Names	Types of Books
000–099	General Works	Encyclopedias and other reference books
100–199	Philosophy and Psychology	Things people think and wonder about
200–299	Religion	Bible stories and mythology
300–399	Social Sciences	Fairy tales, legends, holidays
400–499	Language	Books about languages
500–599	Science	Scientific things that occur naturally
600–699	Technology	Scientific things that are invented or created
700–799	Arts and Recreation	Sports, hobbies and art
800–899	Literature	Poetry, jokes and plays
900–999	History and Geography	History and places

Out of this World · Lesson 6

Featured Book

The Magic School Bus Lost in the Solar System by Joanna Cole. Scholastic, 1990.

On a special field trip in the magic school bus, Ms. Frizzle's class goes into outer space and visits each planet in the solar system. ISBN 0590414283

Lesson Learning Ideas

Library Skills

- Uses multiple resources to locate information

Techniques of Learning

- Has the opportunity to work in cooperative groups

- Attends to personal and/or team tasks outside of the whole group setting

Oral Language

- Is able to listen to and comprehend a variety of multimedia presentation formats

Materials

- *The Magic School Bus Lost in the Solar System* by Joanna Cole

- *The Magic School Bus Explores the Solar System* CD (see Ordering Information, page 151)

- Note from Ms. Frizzle (page 33)

- computer access for CD and/or Internet

Before Class

1. Decide how you would like to present the story segment for this lesson. Show the rest of the video from the last lesson or use *The Magic School Bus Explores the Solar System* CD.

2. Create the note from Ms. Frizzle using the text on page 33.

3. Prepare activities from the Magic School Bus Web site. *(Optional)*

Lesson Plan

1. Greet the class by reading the note left by Ms. Frizzle. The note says:

Dear Students,

I lost my class in outer space! Could you help my students learn more about space so they can locate me? Perhaps you could help them find some good library books about space. I know books are always a good place to start when I need to know something. Just make sure the books are nonfiction. Enjoy your trip to learning!

Ms. Frizzle

2. If possible, allow students to finish the story using *The Magic School Bus Explores the Solar System* CD. If students are using the CD, have them start the program and listen to how it all started for the Friz and her class. Your students will also be introduced to each of the students in Ms. Frizzle's class. When the screen changes to the inside of the school building, listen to Liz talk about the difference between what can happen and what can't really happen. Do not click around as suggested. When the picture enlarges, click on the school bus. Let the screens move on their own. Click on the steering wheel of the spacecraft to go to each of the planets where the Friz might be waiting. At each planet stop and click on the door to get out of the spacecraft. Students can play games on each planet and/or learn information about the planet. Allow students to play through the experience.

3. If the video option is used, simply start the video story where it left off in the last lesson and continue to the end of the video. After the story there are some facts about space and some of the fiction elements in the Magic School Bus story.

4. Share the Scholastic Web site with students to enjoy more activities related to the Magic School Bus books in general and *The Magic School Bus Lost in the Solar System* in particular. The Web site can be found at: *www.scholastic.com/magicschoolbus/*.

Out of this World · Lesson 7

Featured Books

Exploring Space by Toni Eugene. National Geographic Society, 1999.

Explains the different ways we learn about space and shows astronauts at work. ISBN 0792294262

The Visual Dictionary of the Universe by Sue Becklake. DK Publishing, 1993.

Colorful photographs and concise text explain the different features of the universe with clear definitions of the concepts. ISBN 1564583368

Lesson Learning Ideas

Library Skills

- Is familiar with basic reference books and their purpose

- Is able to identify, utilize and create basic parts of a book

Literature Appreciation

- Understands and applies the concepts of fiction and nonfiction

Techniques of Learning

- Uses organizational formats for learning

- Is able to integrate cues from written and visual text

Comprehension

- Has extended personal vocabulary

Materials

- *The Magic School Bus Lost in the Solar System* big book version by Joanna Cole (see Ordering Information, page 151)

- *Exploring Space* big book version by Toni Eugene (see Ordering Information, page 151)

- *The Visual Dictionary of the Universe* or other space dictionary

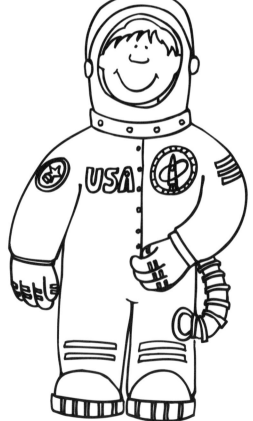

- paper and crayons

- Venn Diagram visual (page 36)

Before Class

1. Post the brainstorm ideas about space from lesson 1.

2. Reproduce the Venn Diagram visual for class use.

Lesson Plan

1. Remind the students that in an earlier lesson they were told that Magic School Bus books were actually three books in one and that the series of books changed nonfiction forever. In this lesson students will have a chance to explore these issues.

2. Share the big book version of *The Magic School Bus Lost in Space* with the students. Introduce the three different books in each MSB book. Read aloud some of the regular text and discuss that the text in this part of the book contains fictional content. A reader could read only the regular text and get a complete story. Draw attention to the dialogue balloons. These provide a second stand-alone story. Focus attention on the fact that some of the content is factual and some is fictional. Finally, look at the third book within this book. This is contained in the science reports shown written on notebook paper. The reports contain only factual information. Use a Venn Diagram visual to show how a MSB book could actually fit in the intersecting segment between fiction and nonfiction on a Venn diagram.

3. Share the big book version of *Exploring Space*. Ask students to decide where this book would fit on the Venn Diagram visual.

4. Use the brainstorm list from lesson 1 to stimulate more words that have to do with space. Encourage the children to use words from the books presented in today's lesson. When the students have exhausted their word ideas assign pairs of students to illustrate one word from the list (save this list of words for a later lesson). Each group should include an explanation of what the word means along with a picture. As students work, circulate and assist students in completing the task.

5. Introduce a space dictionary such as *The Visual Dictionary of the Universe*. Explain the components of a typical entry. As a class, construct a full entry for some of the words the students illustrated and defined. Put the student work in alphabetical order and create a cover, title page and spine label for the student-designed book.

Venn Diagram

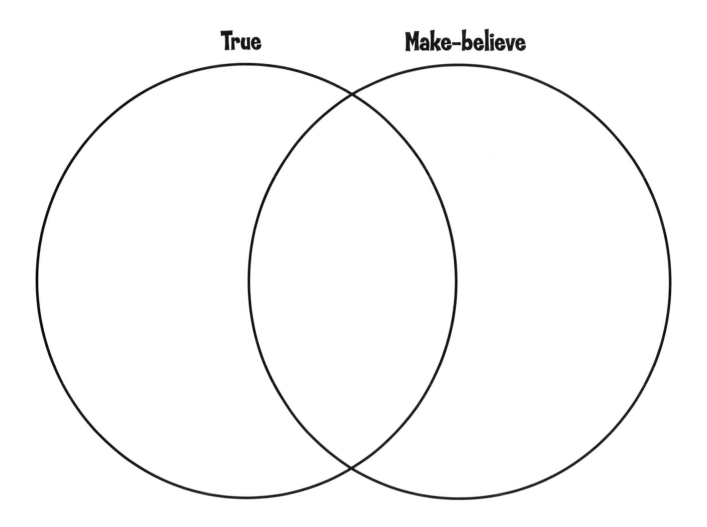

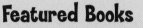

Featured Books

Rabbit and the Moon by Douglas Wood. Simon & Schuster, 1998.
Crane helps Rabbit fulfill his dream of riding across the sky to the moon.
ISBN 0689807694

Lesson Learning Ideas

Techniques of Learning

- Has established visual literacy skills

- Understands and participates in brainstorming activities

- Takes an active role in recomposing visual and written information

- Can appropriately access, evaluate and apply Internet-sourced information

Comprehension

- Is able to make connections with prior knowledge and experience

Materials

- *Rabbit and the Moon* by Douglas Wood

- Internet access

- measuring tape

- string, fishing line or yarn

- globe

- tennis ball, basketball, soccer ball, two softballs, two ping pong balls, ball for playing jacks and two marbles

- roll of adding machine paper or roll of toilet paper

Before Class

1. Gather all the materials.

2. Go over the activities to make sure the directions are clear.

Lesson Plan

1. Read aloud *Rabbit and the Moon.* Show the students a globe and a tennis ball. Explain that these are scale models of the earth and the moon. Ask students: If these are scale models, how far apart should they be to indicate the relative distance between the earth and the moon? Take several guesses, then explain that the distance between the earth and the moon is 9½ times around the earth's equator. Use string, yarn or fishing line to create the distance.

2. Explain to the students that we cannot use these items (globe and tennis ball) if we want to make a scale model of the solar system because there is not enough room. For example, if we used the globe shown for the earth, our scale model sun would have to be large enough to hold 1.3 million globes. Instead they are going to build a solar system two different ways.

3. Use the other balls to compare the relative sizes of the planets. To create a solar system use a basketball for Jupiter; a soccer ball for Saturn; softballs for Uranus and Neptune; ping pong balls for Earth and Venus; a ball for playing jacks for Mars and marbles for Mercury and Pluto. Have the students organize the planets in order.

4. Create a second model solar system based on distance between the planets. Visit the Web site *www.exploratorium.edu/ronh/solar_system/.* Use the basketball to represent the sun instead of Jupiter and enter the diameter (9.55″) of the basketball. Have the calculator create the distances that would need to be used. Show the students that the distance to Pluto would be 3,380 feet or approximately 1,126 yards. Since there are 100 yards on a football field it would take 11-plus football fields end to end to make a scale model of the solar system. Again adjust the sizes of the planets so that they can be seen within a school building. As the Web site suggests, use .4 inches or 10 millimeters for the diameter of the sun. This way the solar system should fit on a roll of adding machine tape or a roll of toilet paper.

Out of this World · Lesson 9

Featured Book

New Pet **by Dan Yaccarino. Hyperion, 2001.**

Both Blast Off Boy, on the planet Meep, as well as Blorp, on Earth, want pets, but neither gets what he expected—at first. ISBN 078680579X

Lesson Learning Ideas

Literature Appreciation

- Has experience with literary based drama

Techniques of Learning

- Can appropriately access, evaluate and apply Internet-sourced information

- Has the opportunity to work in cooperative groups

- Attends to personal and/or team tasks outside of the whole group setting

- Takes an active role in recomposing visual and written information

Writing Experiences

- Has experience with examples of descriptive writing and its uses

- Participates in descriptive writing experiences

Materials

- *New Pet* by Dan Yaccarino

- *New Pet* play script (page 41)

- Reader's Cards (page 42)

- Space Pet Cards (page 43–44), Worksheet (page 45) and Our Space Pet picture (page 46)

- crayons and pencils

- Internet access

- notebook paper and envelopes *(optional)*

Before Class

1. Make a copy of the play for each student.

2. Copy the Reader's Cards on different colored paper. Make one set for every five children.

3. Copy the Space Pet Cards on different colored paper. Make one set for every five children.

4. Copy one Our Space Pet picture for each group

5. Visit the Blast Off Boy Web site at *www.blastoffboy.com* to access the play about the first book in the series, pictures of the characters and/or information to share with students. Prepare any materials to use with students.

Lesson Plan

1. Share the cover of *New Pet*. Tell students that this is the second book in a series about an Earth boy and alien boy exchanging lives. Use the Web site to introduce the characters and provide students with copies of the color pages of the characters. Read the summary of the book. Explain that the class is going to read part of the book that has been re-written in play format. (This is not the play from the Web site.)

2. Divide the students into groups with at least five students in each group. Hand out one set of Reader's Cards and a set of scripts to each group. Have one child at a time draw a card from the Reader's Cards. If they do not like the part they drew they can put it back in the stack, but they must accept the second part even if they draw the same card again. Shuffle the cards after each drawing.

3. Review the following words before student groups start to read: "schloppo," "Meep," "Glorp" and "Yaccarino." Remind students to use their six-inch voices since everyone in the class will be reading the same story at the same time. Allow groups to read the play together.

4. Give students the chance to create their own Space Pet. Hand out the Space Pet Cards, Worksheet, Our Space Pet picture and a set of crayons per group. Instruct the students to allow one person to draw one card at a time. The student who draws the card should read the card contents aloud. Then that student should add to the picture of the pet or the information about their group Space Pet. Cards that have a picture of a crayon indicate the student should draw something while the cards with a pencil and paper mean they should write information on their worksheet. Students must comply with the card they draw. When all the cards have been drawn the group will have constructed their group Space Pet.

5. When all of the groups are finished let the student groups share what they have created.

6. If time allows, review the format of a friendly letter. Go over the five parts in a friendly letter: date, greeting, body, closing and signature. Share examples of friendly letters. Inform the children that they are going to write a friendly letter to their parents as though they lived in outer space like Blast Off Boy, and wanted to tell them about their new pet. Have students select at least three things to tell their parents about their new pet. When the students have completed their letter they should address an envelope using the complete address they created in lesson 2.

New Pet

Adapted from the book by Dan Yaccarino

Readers: Narrator 1; Narrator 2; Blast Off Boy *(an Earth child living on the planet Meep)*; Mrs. Glorp *(Blast Off Boy's mother on Meep)*; Mr. Glorp *(Blast Off Boy's father on Meep)*

Narrator 1:   Blast Off Boy woke so early that there were only two suns in the sky. He opened his sleep pod and floated down to breakfast.

Mrs. Glorp: Good morning, Blast Off Boy. How many breakfast pills would you like this morning?

Blast Off Boy: Only seventeen, please. I'm not that hungry.

Mr. Glorp: We have a BIG surprise for you!

Narrator 2:   Blast Off Boy was startled as a giant, slobbering green monster tackled him and stood on his chest, licking his face.

Blast Off Boy: W-What is this?

Mr. Glorp: Why, your new pet schloppo, of course! We named him Twinkles.

Mrs. Glorp: We thought you'd like a little pet.

Narrator 1:   The big green monster put Blast Off Boy's head in his mouth.

Mr. Glorp: Say, he's taken quite a liking to you!

Blast Off Boy: Are you sure he's not trying to eat me?

Narrator 2:   After school, Blast Off Boy spent the rest of the day trying to teach his new pet to fetch, roll over and sit.

Mrs. Glorp: Why are you trying to teach Twinkles how to do those things?

Blast Off Boy: Because.

Narrator 1:   Blast Off Boy didn't quite know why, but he knew what a good pet was supposed to do.

Narrator 2:   So what is a good pet? Finish reading the book called *New Pet* by Dan Yaccarino to find out about pets on Earth and in outer space.

Narrator 1	Narrator 2
Blast Off Boy	Mrs. Glorp
Mr. Glorp	

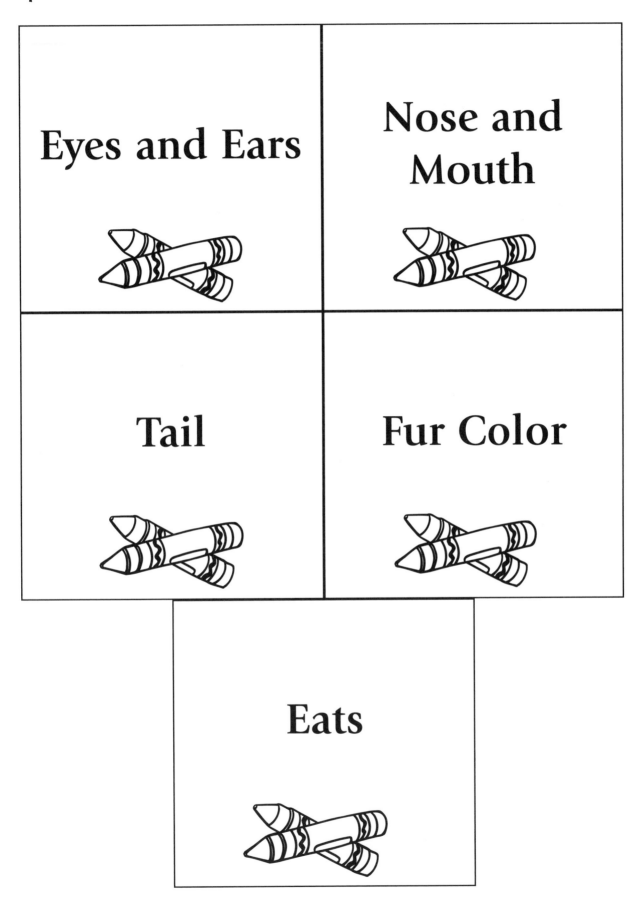

Eyes and Ears

Nose and Mouth

Tail

Fur Color

Eats

Feet

Sleeps

Name of pet

Something it can do an Earth pet can't

Type or kind of animal

Space Pet Worksheet

Our pet likes to eat _____

_____ .

Our pet likes to sleep _____

_____ .

Our pet's name is _____ .

Our pet is a _____ .

Our pet can _____

_____

_____

_____

_____

Our Space Pet

It's Raining Cats and Dogs

It's Raining Cats and Dogs
Lesson 1

Featured Books

The Best Pet of All by David LaRochelle. Penguin Group, 2004.

A young boy enlists the help of a dragon to persuade his mother to let him have a dog as a pet. ISBN 0525471294

Don't Take Your Snake for a Stroll by Karin Ireland. Harcourt, 2003.

Mayhem ensues when a boy takes unusual pets like a rhinoceros and a kangaroo to places usually reserved for people. ISBN 0152023615

No More Monsters for Me! by Peggy Parish. HarperCollins, 1981.

Minneapolis Simpkin is not allowed to have a pet, so she finds the most unusual replacement. ISBN 0060246588

The Perfect Pet by Carol Chataway. Kids Can Press, 2001.

Hamlet, Pygmalion and Podge are three pigs who want a dog, but after trying out several they wonder if they will ever find the perfect pet. ISBN 155337178X

The Perfect Pet by Margie Palatini. HarperCollins, 2003.

After Elizabeth's parents do not agree with her various suggestions for the perfect pet, she discovers a solution. ISBN 0060001097

Lesson Learning Ideas

Techniques of Learning

- Attends to personal and/or team tasks outside of the whole group setting
- Understands and participates in brainstorming activities
- Has the opportunity to work in cooperative groups
- Has experience with compare and contrast questioning

Writing Experiences

- Can create labels, notes and/or captions

Oral Language

- Has taken part in storytelling and read aloud experiences

Materials

- *The Perfect Pet* by Carol Chataway (RL 2.8)
- *Don't Take Your Snake for a Stroll* by Karin Ireland (RL 4.3)
- *The Perfect Pet* by Margie Palatini (RL 4.0)
- *The Best Pet of All* by David LaRochelle (RL 1.3)
- *No More Monsters for Me!* by Peggy Parish (RL 2.7)
- drawing paper and crayons

Before Class

Gather the featured books and review the reading levels to decide if they will be within the reading ability of the students. If they are not, create a cassette tape of the story for students to follow as they read.

Lesson Plan

1. Ask the students what hamsters, guinea pigs, goldfish, cats, dogs and parakeets have in common. Create a list of the things these items have in common. **Hint:** One of the things these items have in common is what the next library unit is about.

2. Divide the class into five groups. Give each group one of the featured books. Explain that reading these books will help them figure out what the next unit will be about. Have the students read their books aloud as a group.

3. When all of the groups have finished reading, allow the students to find someone who did not read the book they read. Give the student pairs time to talk about the books they read. Students can continue to switch partners and discuss as time allows.

4. Bring the children back together as a class. Discuss the topic for the new unit. What evidence did they use to decide the topic of the new unit?

5. Give each student paper and crayons. Ask them to draw a picture of one of the pets from the book they read in their group. Remind the children to label their drawings with the type of pet. Save these pictures for a later lesson.

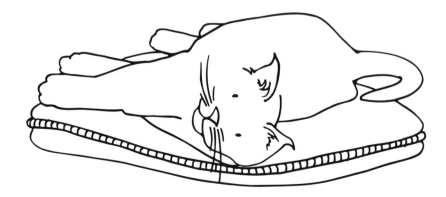

It's Raining Cats and Dogs
Lesson 2

Featured Video

Paws, Claws, Feathers and Fins. Peter Pan Studios, 2002.

A cast of kids guide you in choosing a pet, living with it and dealing with loss. Peter Pan Growing Up Well series. ISBN 0739603736

Lesson Learning Ideas

Techniques of Learning

- Has experience in critical thinking questioning

- Has experience with compare and contrast questioning

- Uses organizational formats for learning

Oral Language

- Is able to listen to and comprehend a variety of oral presentation formats

- Has participated in oral presentation experiences

Materials

- *Paws, Claws, Feathers and Fins* video (see Ordering Information, page 151)

- T-chart visual (page 52)

Before Class

1. Gather the student pictures from Lesson 1.

2. Copy the T-chart visual and attach one to the back of each student picture.

Lesson Plan

1. Have the children discuss what makes a pet a good pet or a bad pet. As a class, brainstorm a list of things that make any pet a good or bad choice.

2. Show the 30-minute *Paws, Claws, Feathers and Fins* video.

3. Give each student the picture they colored in the last lesson. Have the children turn their picture over and look at the T-chart. On one side ask them to list why their animal would be a good pet and on the other side why it would not.

4. Have the students present their pets and arguments. Save this information for the next lesson.

This animal would make a good pet because ...	This animal would not make a good pet because ...

It's Raining Cats and Dogs
Lesson 3

Featured Book

Should We Have Pets? A Persuasive Text by Sylvia Lollis with Joyce Hogan and her second-grade class. Mondo, 2003.

A second-grade class presents arguments for and against pet ownership. ISBN 1590340442

Lesson Learning Ideas

Techniques of Learning

- Takes an active role in recomposing visual and written information

Comprehension

- Is able to make connections with prior knowledge and experience

- Can recall, summarize and paraphrase what is listened to and viewed

- Has experience with reading for the purpose of extending knowledge and understanding

Writing Experiences

- Participates in persuasive writing experiences

- Has experience with examples of persuasive writing and its uses

Oral Language

- Has participated in oral presentation experiences

Materials

- *Should We Have Pets?* by Sylvia Lollis (see Ordering Information, page 151)

- Writing to Be Persuasive worksheet (page 55)

- notebook paper and pencil

- selected pet pictures from lesson 2

Before Class

1. Enlarge the Writing to Be Persuasive chart or make it into a transparency so the whole class will have access to the information at the same time.

2. Select one of the animals from the previous lessons for the class to focus on when making an argument about why it would not be a good pet. Select an animal that the students had strong opinions about during the previous lessons.

Lesson Plan

1. Ask students if they have ever tried to change someone's mind about something. For example, have they ever tried to get their parents to let them do something that their parents said they could not do? Let the children discuss several situations where they tried to persuade someone about something. Explain that when this is done in writing it is called persuasive writing.

2. Share *Should We Have Pets?* by Sylvia Lollis. Read aloud pages 4 and 5, which introduce the concept of persuasive writing. Provide time for student groups to read several of the entries. If this is too difficult for the students the same experience can be accomplished by a whole class read aloud.

3. Bring out the picture of the animal the students will use. Share the information from the T-chart visual created in the last lesson. Brainstorm more reasons why this animal would not be considered a good pet.

4. Introduce the persuasive writing chart. Walk through each step, providing numerous examples and asking students to create examples of their own.

5. Redirect the attention to the animal in question. As a class, create a statement of opinion, three or more elements of proof and some of the reasons it would not be a good pet. Then have student pairs argue their points with each student taking a turn.

6. Give each student a small piece of paper. Ask each student to pick which animal, choosing from a monster, bug or dragon, they think would be the worst pet. Have them secretly write their selection on the paper.

7. Have the students place their paper on their forehead, facing away from their body. Call one animal name at a time and have the children who chose that animal form a group in one corner of the room. When all groups are assembled, give the groups time to talk about their opinions.

Writing to Be Persuasive

1. State your opinion. There are three ways to state your opinion.

   - You can state that something is true or not true. Example: Humans cannot have monsters for a pet.

   - You can state that something does or does not have a certain advantage. Example: Having a bug for a pet means you don't have to worry about it shedding on the carpet.

   - You can state that something should or should not be done. Example: Don't take your snake for a stroll.

2. Use words that help you support your opinion, but try to avoid statements that are all-or-nothing comments. Avoid words like: all, best, every, never, none or worst. Try using: almost, often, usually, sometimes likely, maybe, most, many, probably and frequently.

3. Support your opinion with as much proof as possible. Some sources of proof might come from:

   - **Numbers.** Example: Two-thirds of all households that have a pet have a cat for a pet.

   - **Predictions.** Example: Having a pet will encourage a child to be more responsible.

   - **Experiences.** Example: Three of my friends have had their own dogs for more than a year.

   - **Experts.** Example: Our veterinarian says that a goldfish might be a good pet for me.

   - **Comparisons.** Example: A dog needs more space to play than a cat does.

4. Nothing is perfect so offer answers for as many problems as you can. Use words like: even though, while it is true that, I will admit, I agree that, you're right, I cannot argue and I accept the fact.

5. Find your strongest point and let it be the first or the last point you make in your argument.

It's Raining Cats and Dogs
Lesson 4

Featured Book

Arthur's New Puppy by Marc Brown. Little, Brown and Company, 1993.

Arthur's new puppy causes problems when it tears the living room apart, wets on everything and refuses to wear a leash. ISBN 0316109215

Lesson Learning Ideas

Literature Appreciation

- Has an understanding of how authors write books

Techniques of Learning

- Has established visual literacy skills

- Is able to integrate cues from written and visual text

- Can transfer learning experiences across multiple situations

Comprehension

- Has experience with reading for the purpose of extending knowledge and understanding

Writing Experiences

- Can create labels, notes and/or captions

Materials

- *Arthur's New Puppy* by Marc Brown book and video (see Ordering Information, page 151)

- Pet Pointers visual (page 58)

- drawing paper and colors

- books from your library collection by Marc Brown

Before Class

Convert the Pet Pointers visual into a usable format for whole class use.

Lesson Plan

1. Tell the children that Marc Brown, the author of the Arthur books, got started with stories when he was young. When he was growing up his grandmother told wonderful stories. When he became a father he started telling bedtime stories to his son. Even today Marc Brown makes each of his books a family affair. In each book you will find the names of his children, Tolon, Tucker and Eliza. Their names are hidden in the pictures. Sometimes his wife Laurie's name can be found too. Provide copies of Arthur books and have the children search for the names in the illustrations.

2. Explain that they are going to use one of Marc Brown's books about owning a new pet. Show the cover of *Arthur's New Puppy.* Ask where this book would be found on the shelf. Show the 12-minute video of the book.

3. Share the Pet Pointers visual. Ask the students to think about the Arthur story as you go through the pointers. Read through the pointers and discuss what each covers.

4. Provide copies of the book so that every two or three children have one, or do the activity as a class. Have the children play a visual scavenger hunt. Ask them to look for pictures of things Arthur has to do to take care of his new puppy based on the items listed in the chart. Make a list of the items covered in the story beside each Pet Pointer.

5. Discuss what items in the list were not covered in the story. Have students pick one of the items to create a picture and caption relating how it could be added to the story.

Pet Pointers

Proper food and water. Pets need:

- foods that will not make them sick
- pet food, not people food
- the right amount of food
- different foods at different times in their life
- fresh water

Pets need proper rest and exercise. Their:

- amount of rest changes over time
- amount of exercise and type changes over time

Grooming needs. Pets need:

- baths
- brushing
- their teeth and ears cleaned
- cleaning up after
- their hair and nails clipped

Love and attention. Pets need:

- respect and patience from their humans
- treats and toys that are good for them

Veterinary care. Pets need:

- regular health care
- shots
- medicines to keep them healthy
- care of minor injuries
- to be taken to a veterinarian when they are sick or hurt
- to be spayed or neutered

Proper shelter. Pets need:

- a house to protect them from weather
- a fenced in, safe space to run and play
- a comfortable place to sleep

Training and discipline. Pets need:

- to be housebroken or litter-box trained
- obedience training
- a collar, identification tag and leash

It's Raining Cats and Dogs
Lesson 5

Lesson Learning Ideas

Techniques of Learning

- Has the opportunity to work in cooperative groups

- Understands and participates in brainstorming activities

- Is able to integrate cues from written and visual text

Comprehension

- Is able to make connections with prior knowledge and experience

- Has extended personal vocabulary

- Is beginning to comprehend basic text structures

Materials

- *Mapping Penny's World* by Loreen Leedy

- *Measuring Penny* by Loreen Leedy

- chart paper and markers for student groups

- Post-it® notes

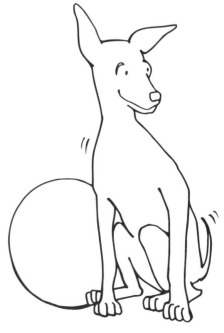

Before Class

Decide how to share the two focus maps from the book *Mapping Penny's World*.

Lesson Plan

1. Begin the lesson by showing Loreen Leedy's two books about Penny. Divide the students into teams of four or five students. Give each team a piece of chart paper and a marker. Set a time limit. Have the students record as many different ways of measuring as they can. When the time is up, make a class list using all of the items from the groups. *Optional:* Divide the items from the brainstorm into standard and nonstandard units.

2. Read aloud *Measuring Penny.* Then go back through the book to find the different types of measuring that are shown. When students identify a way to measure, record the type of measurement on a Post-it® note and stick it on the page. Go back to the book one last time and compare the types of measurements in the book to the class list.

3. Briefly explain the story behind *Mapping Penny's World.* Read the book highlighting the six items included on a map (title, key, symbols, scale, compass rose and labels). Focus on two of the maps—Lisa's bedroom and Penny's Treasure Map. Discuss how Lisa made these maps.

4. Have students locate the six items on each map. This will prepare them for the activity with next week's book.

It's Raining Cats and Dogs Lesson 6

Featured Book

Harry the Dirty Dog by Gene Zion. HarperCollins, 1984.

A little dog runs away because he hates baths. He is so dirty when he returns that no one recognizes him. ISBN 0060268662

Lesson Learning Ideas

Library Skills

- Can locate and identify the basic parts of a book

Literature Appreciation

- Understands the concept of a book series and how they are linked by common characters

Techniques of Learning

- Uses organizational formats for learning
- Takes an active role in recomposing visual and written information

Comprehension

- Is able to make connections with prior knowledge and experience
- Has experience in the comprehension strategy of retelling

Writing Experiences

- Can create labels, notes and/or captions

Materials

- *Harry the Dirty Dog* by Gene Zion book and listening cassette or CD (see Ordering Information, page 151)
- Neighborhood Map (page 63)

Before Class

Make copies of the map for the students to use.

Lesson Plan

1. Dogs are the main character in several book series. Ask the students if they can name any dogs that appear in a series of books. Provide examples of what a series is if students are not familiar with the concept. (Examples: Clifford; Harry, the dirty dog; Martha; Angus; Biscuit; Boomer; Carl; Hairy; Maclary; Kipper; Spot; McDuff; Mudge; and Wishbone.)

2. Share that the main character in today's story has a series of books written about him. (Other books in the series include: *Harry and the Lady Next Door, Harry By the Sea, No Roses for Harry.*) Provide students with copies of *Harry the Dirty Dog* so they can read along as they listen to the story being read.

3. Have the students turn to the verso of the title page to find when this book was published/copyrighted. Help the students figure out how many years ago that was. Explain that some of the places that Harry visited don't exist anymore or don't look like they would if the story were written today.

4. Ask the children to list all of the places that Harry visited using both the text and the pictures. Put the places in the correct sequence, then discuss whether or not each place would be found in their town today.

5. Have the children work as a class or in pairs to follow the map, tracking all of the places that Harry went during the story. Review the six map items from lesson 5. Discuss and create the items that are applicable to this map.

Map Answer Key

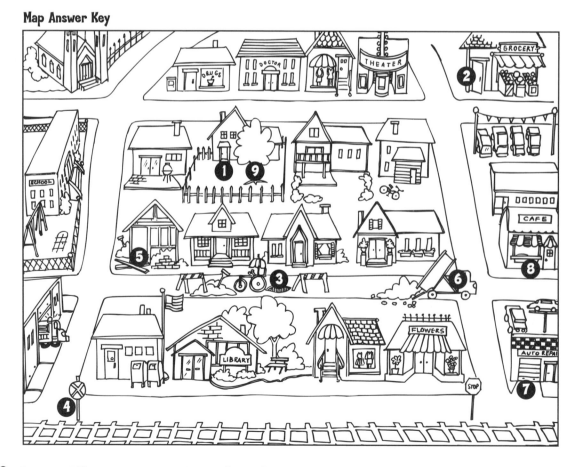

Harry the Dirty Dog's Neighborhood

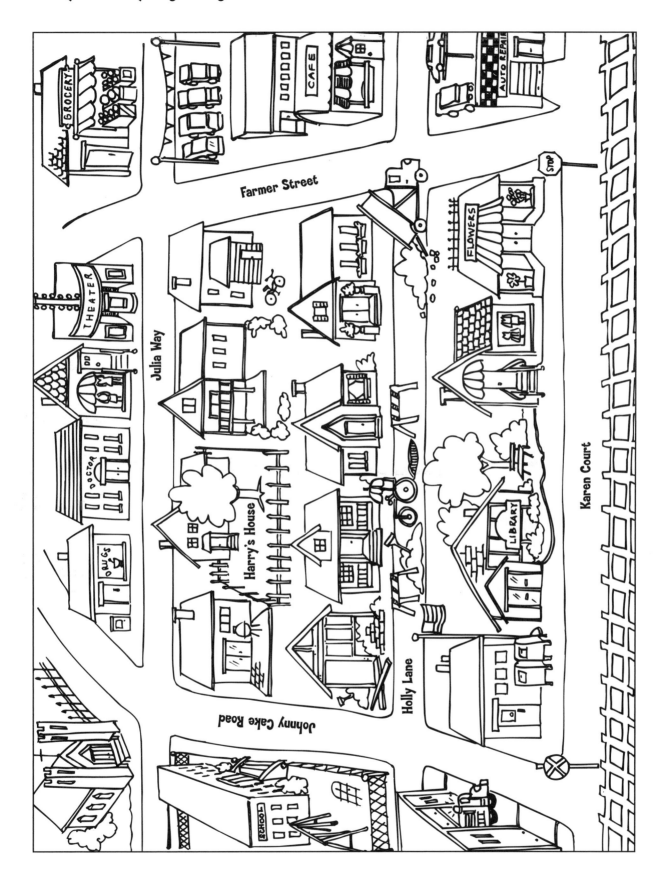

It's Raining Cats and Dogs
Lesson 7

Featured Book

Officer Buckle and Gloria by Peggy Rathmann. Penguin Putnam, 1995.

The children at Napville Elementary School always ignore Officer Buckle's safety tips, until a police dog named Gloria accompanies him when he gives his safety speeches. ISBN 0399226168

Lesson Learning Ideas

Literature Appreciation

- Knows the meaning of award-winning literature

Writing Experiences

- Has experience with examples of narrative writing and its uses

- Is able to transfer ideas into sentences with appropriate support

- Responds to literature in a variety of written formats

- Has experience with examples of expository writing and its uses

- Participates in narrative writing experiences

- Participates in expository writing experiences

Materials

- *Officer Buckle and Gloria* by Peggy Rathmann book and video (see Ordering Information, page 152)

- transparencies of safety tips from book

- notebook paper

- pencils

- crayons

- drawing paper for making posters

- large stars for displaying safety tips from the book *(optional)*

- Sample Children's Letters (page 66)

- Tips for Making Posters worksheet (page 67)

- list of Caldecott Award books

- thank-you notes from featured book

Before Class

1. Make transparencies of the pages from the book that include safety tips as part of the illustrations.

2. Make large stars for students to write down safety tips that they find in the book. Number the stars and laminate them. Use dry erase markers so the stars can be re-used with several classes. *(Optional)*

3. Create presentation methods for the Sample Children's Letters and the Tips for Making Posters worksheet so that they will be visible to the whole class.

Lesson Plan

1. Share a copy of *Officer Buckle and Gloria*. Have the students locate the copyright/publication date of this book. Assist the students in figuring out how much older *Harry the Dirty Dog* is. *Officer Buckle and Gloria* won the Caldecott Award in 1996. Books can only win in the first year after publication. Have the students figure out what year Harry would have been eligible to win the Caldecott Award. Check a list to see what book won for that year. *(A Tree is Nice)*

2. Watch the *Officer Buckle and Gloria* 11-minute video.

3. Draw the children's attention to the notes the students at Napville School wrote to Officer Buckle and Gloria. Share that there are many kinds of notes that people write. The children in the book wrote thank-you notes for Officer Buckle and Gloria.

4. Share the Sample Children's Letters provided. As a class, ask the students to come up with a list of tips about writing notes. For example, notes are usually very short, only a few sentences long. Save this information for later in the lesson.

5. Shift the attention to the safety tips by doing a safety tip search using the book. The book talks about 101 safety tips. Start by collecting the safety tips listed on the endpapers (notice that one of the tips is listed twice). Use the five pages from the story that show safety tips as part of the illustrations. Place each tip on a star *(optional)*. When these tips have been collected, do the math to see how many more would be needed to reach 101. Let students add their own safety tips so the list will reach 101.

6. Show students the Tips for Making Posters worksheet. Explain that posters are sort of like big notes but with less words and more illustration. Provide examples of student-made posters to help students visualize the process.

7. Allow students to create a thank-you note for Officer Buckle and Gloria as though they visited their school or create a poster about a safety tip. Display the children's work for everyone to enjoy.

Sample Children's Letters

Dear Gloria and Officer Buckle,

Thanks for coming
to our school.
You are nice.

Your friend,
George

Dear Gloria and
        Officer Buckle,

Here is a picture of Gloria.
I hope you come back soon.

Your friend,

        Maggie

Dear Officer Buckle and
        Gloria,

My aunt has a dog and she
named him after me. I like
dogs and safety.

Your friend,
Andrew

Dear Officer Buckle and Gloria,

Thank you for coming to our
school to teach us about
safety. When I grow up I
want to be a dog trainer.

Your friend,
        Joe

Tips for Making Posters

1. Make a list of all the things you want to say.

2. Pick the most important fact or facts to make into a picture.

3. Plan your poster before you start to draw.

4. Draw your picture and print your words in pencil.

5. Use the whole piece of paper for your poster.

6. Have someone check your spelling and information.

7. Add color and/or texture to your poster.

It's Raining Cats and Dogs
Lesson 8

Lesson Learning Ideas

Literature Appreciation

- Has had experience with various literary genres

- Has an initial understanding of the difference between fiction and nonfiction

- Understands and applies the concepts of fiction and nonfiction

Writing Experiences

- Has experience with examples of descriptive writing and its uses

- Participates in descriptive writing experiences

- Is able to generate brief descriptions that use sensory details

Oral Language

- Participates in audience participation story-telling

Materials

- *I Am the Dog, I Am the Cat* by Donald Hall

- *A Pet for Me: Poems* selected by Lee Bennett Hopkins

Before Class

1. Create a chart or read-along version of *I Am the Dog, I Am the Cat.*

2. Find someone to read the poem with you during class or prepare a tape with two people reading the parts of the dog and the cat.

3. Select the poems to use with the children. They will be illustrating the poems.

Lesson Plan

1. Present *I Am the Dog, I Am the Cat* using two different readers. As the poem is read share the illustrations that correspond to the text. Explain that this book is sometimes classified as a nonfiction book under the Dewey number 811 and sometimes as an Easy book. Ask students to prove both ways of classifying this book.

2. Divide the class into two groups. Assign one group to read the dog part and one to read the cat part. Allow the students to read along with the presentation readers.

3. Present other selected poems from *A Pet for Me: Poems* but do not share the illustrations. Have each student choose one poem to illustrate.

4. Have the class experience writing a poem about a pet. Choose one of the dog characters presented in the books so far in this unit. Use the book to fill in the following poem form:

Line 1 – the name of the pet
Line 2 – the kind of animal
Line 3 – three words to describe what it looks like
Line 4 – who really likes
Line 5 – who feels
Line 6 – who needs
Line 7 – who gives
Line 8 – who is afraid of or does not like
Line 9 – who makes me
Line 10 – who lives
Line 11 – name of pet

An example using the cat from *Annie and the Wild Animals*:

Taffy is Annie's pet.

Taffy is an ordinary house cat.

Taffy is a soft, cuddly ball of fur.

Taffy really likes to curl up in strange places.

Taffy feels sleepy all day long.

Taffy needs more to eat.

Taffy gives Annie something to worry about during the winter.

Taffy does not like to play anymore.

Taffy makes Annie feel lonely when she doesn't come home.

Taffy lived in the woods all winter.

Taffy—"I am glad you are home!" said Annie.

It's Raining Cats and Dogs
Lesson 9

Featured Book

Annie and the Wild Animals by Jan Brett. Houghton Mifflin, 1985.

When Annie's cat disappears, she attempts friendship with a variety of unsuitable woodland animals, but with the emergence of spring, everything comes out all right. ISBN 0395378001

Lesson Learning Ideas

Techniques of Learning

- Has experience with compare and contrast questioning

- Can appropriately access, evaluate and apply Internet-sourced information

Comprehension

- Utilizes the comprehension strategy of prediction

- Has the opportunity to apply the comprehension strategy of story structure

- Is able to make connections with prior knowledge and experience

- Has the opportunity to participate in experiences that support the acquisition of fluency

Writing Experiences

- Indicates an understanding of story structure necessary for narrative writing

Oral Language

- Is able to listen to and comprehend a variety of oral presentation formats

Materials

- *Annie and the Wild Animals* by Jan Brett

- Internet access

- LPs for *Annie and the Wild Animals* (pages 72–74)

- drawing paper

- crayons

- world map
- Velcro apron or metal board

Before Class

1. Construct the Literature Pictures for *Annie and the Wild Animals.* Follow the directions on page 10.

2. Visit the Jan Brett Web site *(www.janbrett.com)* to select items to use with students. See step 7 below.

Lesson Plan

1. Show the cover of *Annie and the Wild Animals.* Ask the students to predict the setting or location of the story. Show some of the illustrations, but do not share any of the story or the pictures at the end of the book. Explain that this story was written to take place in a part of the world called Scandinavia. Use a map to show the children where Norway, Sweden and Denmark are located. These countries make up the region known as Scandinavia. Compare the location with where the children live. Is it colder, hotter or about the same as in Scandinavia?

2. Tell the story using the LPs on a Velcro apron or metal board. Afterwards, ask the students to list the animals in the story. Use the LP pieces to help if needed.

3. Tell the students that they are going to adapt the story to fit where they live. Describe how they will do this. Talk about how Annie would be dressed on a winter day in the area where the children live. Make a list of the articles of clothing the children think she would be wearing.

4. Create a list of wild animals that live near where the children live. From the list, have the children choose animals that fit the storyline. One animal should be too big, one too mean, one too grumpy and one or more who are not soft and friendly.

5. Have the children decide what kind of food a child would put out for the animals, just like Annie put out the corn cakes.

6. Have students create their own LPs of the story by drawing Annie, the animals and the food they selected. Provide time for the students to tell their version of the story.

7. Use some of the many wonderful materials on Jan Brett's Web site to complete this lesson. Be sure and use the "Jan Brett at Home" video as she tells where the door in the story of Annie came from. In addition, a search using "Annie and the Wild Animals" on an adult search engine will generate numerous Web sites with teaching ideas. These are good to share with classroom teachers to supplement the library lesson.

Literature Pictures (LPs) for Annie and the Wild Animals

Photocopy to desired size.

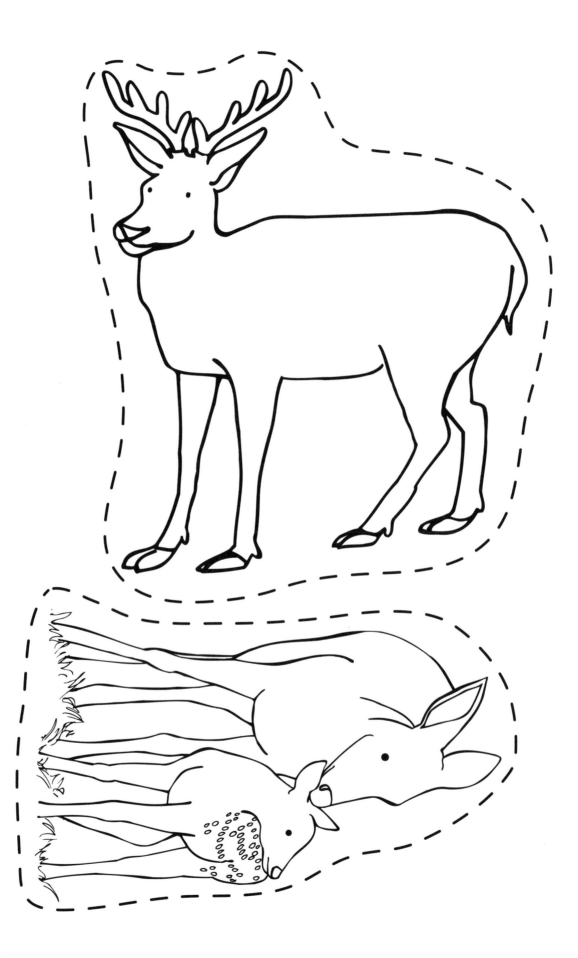

It's Raining Cats and Dogs
Lesson 10

Featured Book

Clarence the Copy Cat by Patricia Lakin. Random House, 2002.

Clarence, a cat who does not want to hurt mice or any other creatures, does not feel welcome anywhere until he discovers the Barnstable Library. ISBN 0385908547

Lesson Learning Ideas

Techniques of Learning

- Uses organizational formats for learning

Writing Experiences

- Has experience with examples of persuasive writing and its uses
- Uses prewriting strategies such as drawings, brainstorming and/or graphic organizers
- Imitates models of good writing
- Participates in persuasive writing experiences

Materials

- *Clarence the Copy Cat* by Patricia Lakin
- Book Report Data Grid and Book Report Frame (pages 77–78)
- book reviews

Before Class

1. Locate the following book reviews based on the featured book:
   - *Booklist*, November 1, 2002
   - *Horn Book*, Spring, 2003
   - *School Library Journal*, October 1, 2002
   - *Kirkus Review*, October 1, 2002
   - *Publishers Weekly*, September 30, 2002

These reviews can be accessed by logging on to *www.titlewave.com* and searching under the book title.

2. Make copies of the Book Report Frame and The Book Report Data Grid for student and class use.

Lesson Plan

1. Read aloud *Clarence the Copy Cat.*

2. Describe how a librarian selects the books that are available in the library. Show some of the review sources used to select the books in the library. These reviews are most often written by librarians, but share the fact that all readers have opinions about the books they read.

3. Share some of the reviews of the featured book. Help the children understand that not all opinions are the same.

4. Introduce the Book Report Data Grid. Walk through the items and use one or more of the reviews to see which items can be found in the published reviews. Have the students fill in the information on the data grid for the book from this lesson as the class talks through the information.

5. When the grid is complete, present the book report writing frame. Demonstrate how to use the frame by taking information from the grid to fill in the blanks in the form. Explain that students can create their own version of a book report/review.

6. Allow time for students to complete the book report/review. If time permits, have students share their reports with other students.

Book Report Data Grid

Title of the book: _____

Author of the book: _____

Section of the library where this book was found *(circle one)*:

       fiction   **nonfiction**   **biography/autobiography**

Main character in story: _____

Other important characters: _____

_____

_____

_____

Three major things that happened to the main character:

_____

_____

_____

Setting—where did the action in the story take place: _____

_____

This book is:

_____ **Fiction**—funny, mystery, realistic, historical, scary, adventure, tall tale or cumulative story

_____ **Nonfiction**—poetry, jokes and riddles, fairy tale, science, history, sports, play, nature or holidays

_____ **Biography** or **Autobiography**

Why did you like this book? *(circle all that fit)*

happy, interesting, true, make-believe, real, funny, sad, scary, adventurous,

fun, unbelievable, like my life, not like my life, surprising

Book Report Frame

The book I just finished reading is called _____

_____

by _____.

The story was about (who) _____,

and what happened when _____

_____.

The story took place in (where) _____

_____.

The story showed how (who) _____

(did what) _____

_____.

In addition, the story showed how (who) _____

(did what) _____

_____.

This book is a (type) _____ book.

I liked this book because it was _____

_____.

So if you like (type) _____ books you will

certainly like reading (title) _____

found in the (where) _____

section of the library.

     © 2005 by Karen A. Farmer Wanamaker (UpstartBooks)

It's Raining Cats and Dogs
Lesson 11

Featured Book

My Nine Lives by Marjorie Priceman. Simon & Schuster, 1998.

The journal of a cat recounting all nine of the lives she has lived and her remarkable effect on history, beginning in Mesopotamia in 3000 BC and culminating in Wisconsin in 1995. ISBN 0689811357

Lesson Learning Ideas

Library Skills

- Is familiar with basic reference books and their purpose

Literature Appreciation

- Has had experience with various literary genres

Techniques of Learning

- Can transfer learning experiences across multiple situations

Writing Experiences

- Has experience with examples of narrative writing and its uses

- Participates in narrative writing experiences

Materials

- *My Nine Lives* by Clio, a.k.a. Marjorie Priceman

- container of Nine Lives® cat food

- notebook

- construction paper

- stapler and/or yarn

- pencils

- crayons

- Internet access and/or a Dictionary of Phrase and Fable

Before Class

1. Obtain a container of Nine Lives® cat food.

2. Use a search engine to locate Web sites with information about the concept that cats have nine lives. Search on the phrase "cats have nine lives."

3. Create a model of a journal so students can visualize the finished product during the instruction.

Lesson Plan

1. Show the children the container of cat food. Ask why a cat food company might name its pet food "Nine Lives." Share the information from the dictionary and/or the Internet describing where this phrase came from.

2. Read aloud the introductory pages of *My Nine Lives*, as well as entries from some of Clio's lives. Be sure to include Life #4 and the information about runes from the back of the book so that the students can try to figure out what is written in the pictures.

3. Ask the students what you would call writing that is done concerning a person's or cat's life where there are entries for different dates. If students are not familiar with the concept of diaries and journals, briefly describe their function.

4. Give students construction paper and notebook paper so they can make their own journal. Provide time for the students to write and draw in their journal. If the children have a difficult time coming up with something to write and draw, suggest one of the following topics:

   • If you had nine lives, in what other time or place would you like to have lived?

   • Share your feelings about your pets, including something funny they have done.

   • Select one or more of the books you have read about pets and tell something about them.

   • If you could create a new pet what would it be like?

It's Raining Cats and Dogs
Lesson 12

Featured Book

Have You Seen My Cat? by Eric Carle. Simon & Schuster, 1987.

A young boy encounters all sorts of cats while searching for the one he lost.
ISBN 0887080545

Lesson Learning Ideas

Library Skills

- Can locate and identify the basic parts of a book

Literature Appreciation

- Understands and applies nonfiction reading techniques

Techniques of Learning

- Has experience with compare and contrast questioning

- Can appropriately access, evaluate and apply Internet-sourced information

Comprehension

- Is able to make connections with prior knowledge and experience

- Is able to set a purpose for reading

Oral Language

- Participates in audience participation storytelling

Materials

- Internet access

- *Have You Seen My Cat?* by Eric Carle

- reference materials on house cats and wild cats

Before Class

1. Make copies of the pictures of the cats from the endpapers of the book.

2. Make a card with the name of each cat on it from *Have You Seen My Cat?*

3. Gather books, reference books and magazines from your library collection that pertain to house cats and wild cats.

4. Find and bookmark the Kids Click search engine at *sunsite.berkeley.edu/KidsClick!/*.

Lesson Plan

1. Have the class read aloud from *Have You Seen My Cat?* Assign half of the class to read the question and the other half to read the answer. Before reading, encourage students to study the pictures carefully.

2. Without using the information on the endpapers, see if the students can match the cat pictures to the correct name cards. Check by using the pictures and text on the endpapers.

3. Explain what endpapers are for and suggest that students look for other books that make use of this extra space.

4. Return to the pictures of the cats from the featured book. Ask students to think of a way to group the cats. Make a list of all of the student suggestions. If no one suggests grouping them by wild cats and house cats extend the discussion. Suggest that one of the cats could form a group by itself. Ask the children if they can find the one that is different.

5. Use multiple resources and student knowledge to develop a list of as many kinds of wild cats and as many kinds of house cats as possible.

6. Introduce the children's search engine called Kids Click! Have students search on the key word "cats." Show the children how to read an entry from this search engine including: the summary of the Web site content, reading level and illustrations. Use the Web site addresses to find information to add to the lists that were started. Before students start searching on the Web, help them decide which Web sites would probably be the best ones to find the information they want.

It's Raining Cats and Dogs
Lesson 13

Featured Book

No featured materials are needed for this lesson.

Lesson Learning Ideas

Library Skills

- Uses multiple resources to locate information

Literature Appreciation

- Understands and applies nonfiction reading techniques

Techniques of Learning

- Uses organizational formats for learning

- Takes an active role in recomposing visual and written information

Comprehension

- Is able to set a purpose for reading

- Has experience with reading for the purpose of extending knowledge and understanding

Writing Experiences

- Uses prewriting strategies such as drawings, brainstorming and/or graphic organizers

Materials

- reading level appropriate materials concerning house cats

- Data Bank form (page 85)

Before Class

1. Gather books from the 636.8 section of your collection.

2. Create class and student copies of the Data Bank form.

Lesson Plan

1. Give students time to browse the materials concerning house cats.

2. Introduce the Data Bank form by going over the categories and explaining the icons; the icons help students who can't read the words, for example, everything a person "has" goes in a suitcase when they travel. Explain that in this lesson, the students will search for information on each of the categories in the Data Bank about house cats. This information will be saved to use with facts found in lesson 14 on wild cats. Also let them know that all of this knowledge will be put together in a research report on cats.

3. Direct the class to search for facts about where house cats live.* As students locate facts, add them to the class Data Bank form. When at least three facts have been located, direct the students' attention to the other topics on the Data Bank sheet.

4. Assign different groups of students to look for facts concerning one other topic from the Data Bank form. Allow the students time to search. Bring the students back to the whole group setting. Fill in as many facts on the Data Bank visual as possible. Save this information for upcoming lessons.

* Direct students to check the table of contents to find chapters that would most likely provide the information needed. They should read the chapters starting with the one selected as having the most potential and working down.

Data Bank for a _____

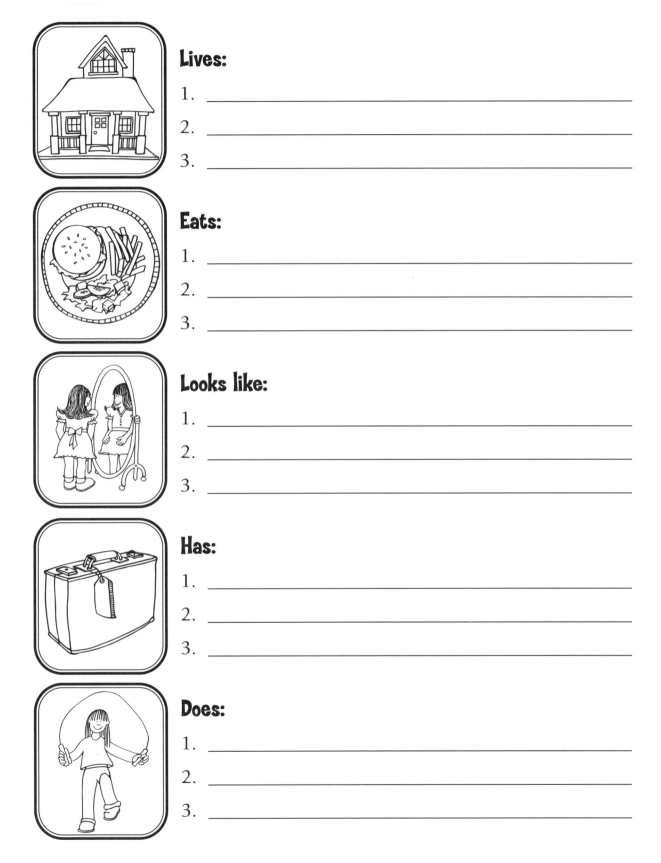

Lives:

1. _____

2. _____

3. _____

Eats:

1. _____

2. _____

3. _____

Looks like:

1. _____

2. _____

3. _____

Has:

1. _____

2. _____

3. _____

Does:

1. _____

2. _____

3. _____

Data Bank adapted with permission from *Research Reports to Knock Your Teacher's Socks Off!*
by Nancy Polette. Pieces of Learning, 1997.

It's Raining Cats and Dogs

It's Raining Cats and Dogs
Lesson 14

Featured Books

Cheetahs by Stephanie St. Pierre. Heinemann Library, 2001.

Presents photographs and information about cheetahs, looking at where they live, their families and behaviors, eating and hunting habits and the dangers they face. ISBN 1588101061

Jaguars by Stephanie St. Pierre. Heinemann Library, 2001.

Includes bibliographical references and index. Presents photographs and information about Jaguars, looking at where they live, their families and behaviors, eating and hunting habits and the dangers they face. ISBN 1588101088

Siberian Tigers by Stephanie St. Pierre. Heinemann Library, 2001.

Includes bibliographical references and index. Presents photographs and information about Siberian tigers, looking at where they live, their families and behaviors, eating and hunting habits and the dangers they face. ISBN 158810110X

Lesson Learning Ideas

Library Skills

- Is developing a basic concept of the research process

Literature Appreciation

- Understands and applies nonfiction reading techniques

Techniques of Learning

- Has the opportunity to work in cooperative groups

Comprehension

- Is beginning to comprehend basic text structures

- Is able to set a purpose for reading

Writing Experiences

- Uses prewriting strategies such as drawings, brainstorming, and/or graphic organizers

Materials

- *Cheetahs* by Stephanie St. Pierre (see Ordering Information, page 152)

- *Jaguars* by Stephanie St. Pierre (see Ordering Information, page 152)

- *Siberian Tigers* by Stephanie St. Pierre (see Ordering Information, page 152)

- Data Bank form (page 85)

Note: Any books on wild cats can be used for this lesson, but this series by Heinemann Library has been written so that the format of every book in the series is the same. This makes it easier to have multiple groups working on different topics at the same time.

Before Class

1. If possible, provide multiple copies of the books.

2. Make copies of the Data Bank worksheet for groups to use during the class.

Lesson Plan

1. Do this lesson as a class or divide the class into three groups.

2. Have the students select one of the wild cats (tiger, jaguar or cheetah) that appeared in *Have You Seen My Cat?*

3. Go over the Data Bank categories. Remind the students of the procedure followed in lesson 13 for locating information.

4. Have the groups locate facts for the Data Bank category on "Lives" for their animal. When the groups locate the facts for their animal, have students share the information with the class.

5. Hand out Data Bank forms to each group. Have the children fill in the information for the first category. Then have them move on to the other categories. Remind the students how dividing up the search process in the last lesson made the work easier.

6. Save the information generated by the groups to use in the next lesson to create a research report.

It's Raining Cats and Dogs
Lesson 15

Lesson Learning Ideas

Writing Experiences

- Has experience with examples of expository writing and its uses

- Participates in expository writing experiences

- Has participated in a variety of age-appropriate writing experiences

- Imitates models of good writing

- Is able to transfer ideas into sentences with appropriate support

Materials

- Research Report Writing Frame (page 89)

- Data Bank information on house cats and wild cats

Before Class

1. Create copies of the Research Report Writing Frame for class and/or student use.

2. Post the information from the Data Bank forms so students can easily make use of the facts.

Lesson Plan

1. Review the information on all of the Data Bank worksheets. Share a copy of the Research Report Writing Frame with the entire class.

2. Create one report as a class or in groups. Prompt students to include pictures with every few sentences to extend the meaning of the text (use the Heinemann Library books' format as a model). In addition, students could use illustrations obtained from Web sites from the Kids Click! search engine at *sunsite.berkeley.edu/KidsClick!/*.

3. Allow time for students to share their reports with others. A display of student reports creates a positive feeling about the work that was done.

Research Report Writing Frame

If I were a _____

I would _____

and I would _____.

If I were a _____

I could _____

and I might _____.

But I wouldn't _____

and I couldn't _____.

Because a house cat does that, not a

_____.

Adapted with permission from *Research Reports to Knock Your Teacher's Socks Off!*
by Nancy Polette, available from Pieces of Learning, 1997, www.piecesoflearning.com.

Duck Fever

Duck Fever • Lesson 1

Featured Book

Make Way for Ducklings by Robert McCloskey. Viking, 1941.

Mr. and Mrs. Mallard proudly return to their home in the Boston Public Garden with their eight offspring. ISBN 0670451495

Lesson Learning Ideas

Library Skills

- Is familiar with basic reference books and their purpose

Literature Appreciation

- Knows the meaning of award-winning literature

Techniques of Learning

- Can appropriately access, evaluate and apply Internet-sourced information

- Is able to integrate cues from written and visual text

Comprehension

- Utilizes the comprehension strategy of prediction

- Can recall, summarize and paraphrase what is listened to and viewed

- Is beginning to comprehend basic text structures

Materials

- *Make Way for Ducklings* by Robert McCloskey (multiple paperback copies if possible)

- Mrs. Mallard Map (page 95)

- pictures and information from suggested Web sites

- *Make Way for Ducklings* video (see Ordering Information, page 152)

Before Class

1. Make copies of the Mrs. Mallard Map for student and class use.

2. Locate the pictures and other information on the Web sites listed in step 6 of the Lesson Plan. If these sites are unavailable, use a search engine and the key words "Boston" and/or "Boston Public Garden."

Lesson Plan

1. Explain to the children that they are going to write a nonfiction book. To help them create a foundation to write, they are going to start with a fiction book.

2. Show the cover of *Make Way for Ducklings.* Ask the children to predict facts about this book and its story from the cover. Students should observe that this is a Caldecott Award book and that the pictures of the cars show that this story took place a long time ago. Ask the students how to find out when this book won the Caldecott Award. The students can look for the copyright date and know that the book had to win the award the year after it was published.

3. Show the *Make Way for Ducklings* 11-minute video.

4. Give copies of the book to small groups of students. Tell the students that this time when they hear the story they should listen for the names of places in the story. Read aloud the first three pages of the book. Ask students to list the places mentioned so far in the story (woods, water, Boston, Public Garden, pond, island). Proceed with the entire story, creating a list of geographical terms along the way.

5. When the story is finished, ask the children why they think some of the terms begin with capital letters. When this has been established, divide the list into geographical terms and names of specific locations.

6. Share with the students that the specific locations are actual places in Boston, Massachusetts, and that the story made the Boston Public Garden so famous that statues of the ducks now stand in the garden. In addition, each year on Mother's Day the city of Boston has a parade through the streets of Boston using the route Mrs. Mallard and her ducklings took in the story. Visit ***www.boston-online.com/cityviews/ducklings_parade.html*** to see pictures of the parade. Visit ***www.freefoto.com*** to find numerous pictures of the statues and the public garden.

7. Give each small group (two or three students) a copy of the Mrs. Mallard Map. Show the students where the island in the Charles River is located. Have the children retrace the steps of the duck family. Along the way, allow the students to locate and label each of the specific locations from the story.

8. If time permits, have the children create a picture geographical dictionary using all of the geographic terms from the story. Students can make use of the pictures in the book to help with their drawings and definitions.

Mrs. Mallard Map

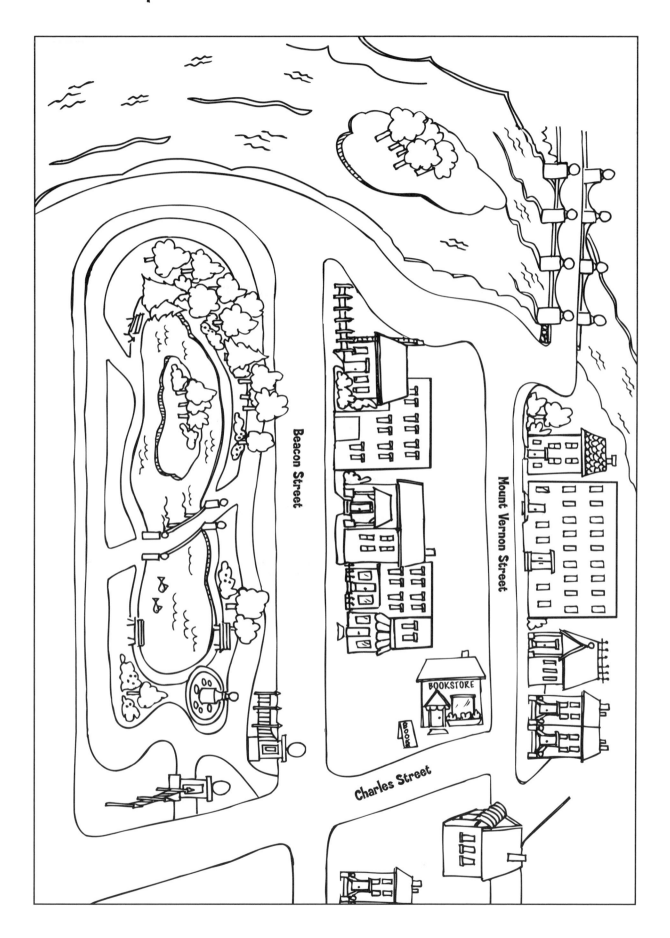

Duck Fever • Lesson 2

Featured Book

Make Way for Ducklings by Robert McCloskey. Viking, 1976.

Mr. and Mrs. Mallard proudly return to their home in the Boston Public Garden with their eight offspring. ISBN 0670451495

Lesson Learning Ideas

Techniques of Learning

- Can transfer learning experiences across multiple situations

- Has the opportunity to work in cooperative groups

Comprehension

- Can recall, summarize and paraphrase what is listened to and viewed

- Is developing the ability to generate appropriate questions

Materials

- *Make Way for Ducklings* by Robert McCloskey (multiple copies if possible)

- Question Stems visual (page 98)

- yarn or painters' tape

- Read-Write-Draw poster (page 99)

- index cards and pencils

- set of large "X" and "O" cards to play tic-tac-toe

Before Class

1. Enlarge the Read-Write-Draw poster.

2. Using index cards, create four or five of each "X" and "O" cards for tic-tac-toe.

3. Create Question Stem cards.

Lesson Plan

Note: *Make Way for Ducklings* is part of the Reading Counts and the Accelerated Reader Program. Perhaps this book could be used as a whole group test as a way of introducing the good comprehension skills needed to be successful with these programs.

1. Share the Read-Write-Draw poster. Explain that whenever the students read, they should stop periodically to write and/or draw about what they read. This will help them remember what they read. This is one of the techniques that good readers use.

2. Show the students the Question Stems visual. These question stems represent knowledge-based questions about any topic. Almost all of the questions used in the AR or RC tests use these question stems. Explain that when students want to check what they know, creating and answering questions based on these question stems is an excellent tool for their good reader toolbox.

3. Select one of the question stem cards and create a question based on that stem. An example might be:
   - Question Stem—Where/When did?
   - Question—Where did Mr. and Mrs. Mallard build their nest?
   - Answer—On an island in the Charles River

4. Break the students into small groups and assign each group a different set of pages to use to create questions. There are 33 pages of text in this book. If this is beyond the ability of the group, the same activity can be done as a class activity. Record each question on a separate index card.

5. Create a giant tic-tac-toe board on the floor using yarn or painters' tape. Divide the students into two teams and play tic-tac-toe using the book questions the students created. In order for a team to place an "X "or an "O" on the board they must answer a book question correctly. Students answer the questions one at a time. If one team cannot answer the question, then the next person in line for the other team gets a chance. When a team answers correctly a member sits in the spot on the board and holds the "X" or "O" card. Play continues until one team has three in a row.

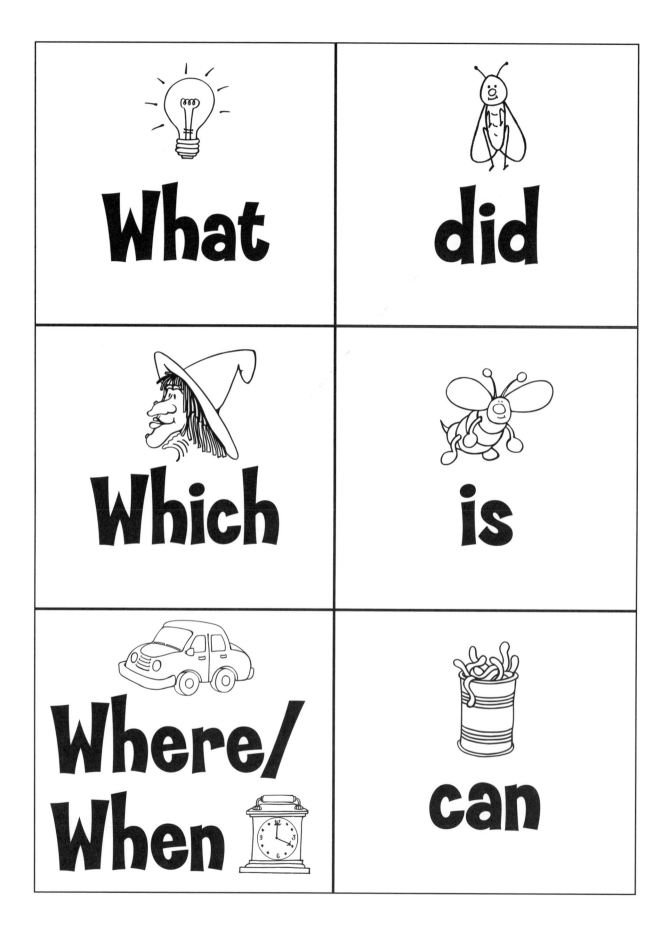

Duck Fever • Lesson 3

Featured Book

Make Way for Ducklings by Robert McCloskey. Viking, 1976.

Mr. and Mrs. Mallard proudly return to their home in the Boston Public Garden with their eight offspring. ISBN 0670451495

Lesson Learning Ideas

Library Skills

- Can utilize alphabetical order as needed for location purposes

Literature Appreciation

- Has an understanding of the concept of artist and illustrator

Techniques of Learning

- Has the opportunity to work in cooperative groups

- Is able to integrate cues from written and visual text

Comprehension

- Has experience in the comprehension strategy of retelling

- Can recall, summarize and paraphrase what is listened to and viewed

Materials

- *Make Way for Ducklings* by Robert McCloskey (multiple copies if possible)

- Duckling Name Cards (page 102)

- Story Event Cards (pages 103–105)

- Numbered Cards (page 106)

- Internet access

- paper

- crayons

Before Class

1. Locate information on the Internet to use with the lesson (see the Web sites in step 1 in the Lesson Plan).

2. Reproduce Duckling Name Cards, Story Event Cards and Numbered Cards as needed to implement the lesson plans.

Lesson Plan

1. Share the interview with Robert McCloskey from *www.hbook.com/exhibit/mccloskey radio.html.* Students can listen to the tape of the interview via the Internet. Other information about Robert McCloskey can be found at *falcon.jmu.edu/~ramseyil/mccloskey.htm.*

2. Introduce the children to two games related to the book. The first one is the "Name Game." Give a set of Duckling Name Cards to small groups of two or three students. Remind them that Robert McCloskey said he created the names in alphabetical order so that the last name was Quack. At the signal, have the students turn their name cards over and put them in alphabetical order. When time is called, check to see how many teams were able to place the names in order. Use the book to check if necessary.

3. The second game is called "What Time Is It?" Before explaining the game, give out copies of the book. Ask students over how much time the action/events in the story took place. Did the action/events take a few days, a few weeks, a few months or a few years? Suggest the students look closely at the trees pictured in the story.

4. Give out the Story Event Cards. Give one card to every two or three students. Read the cards aloud to make sure the students can read the information on their card. Explain that the students will read the book again. This time only the pictures will be shown. When a picture is shown that matches their card, the students should raise their hands. As the cards are gathered, place them in order and use the number cards to indicate their correct sequence.

5. When the story is complete, return the cards to the students who held them before the game. Give each group drawing paper and colors. Have the students illustrate the event indicated by the card they hold. Put the pictures and event cards together to use in a later lesson.

Duckling Name Cards

Story Event Cards

Mr. and Mrs. Mallard were looking for a place to live.	Mr. and Mrs. Mallard spend the night in the Public Garden.
First, Mrs. Mallard decides they should build a nest in the Public Garden and then she changes her mind.	Mr. and Mrs. Mallard continue to search Boston for a perfect place to build a nest.
Finally, Mr. and Mrs. Mallard pick an island in the Charles River on which to build their nest.	Mr. and Mrs. Mallard meet Michael, the policeman.

Mrs. Mallard lays eight eggs.	When the ducklings hatch they are named Jack, Kack, Lack, Mack, Nack, Ouack, Pack and Quack.
Mr. Mallard takes a trip to see the rest of the river.	Mrs. Mallard teaches her ducklings about being ducks.
One day Mrs. Mallard leads the ducklings across the river to the shore.	Michael stops the traffic so the ducks can cross the street.

Michael calls Clancy at police headquarters to help the ducks.	Mrs. Mallard and the ducklings walk down the streets of Boston.
Four policemen hold traffic back so the ducks can cross the street into the Public Garden.	Mr. Mallard meets the ducklings in the Public Garden.
The ducklings decide to live in the Public Garden.	

1	2	3
4	5	6
7	8	9
10	11	12
13	14	15
16	17	

Duck Fever • Lesson 4

Lesson Learning Ideas

Techniques of Learning

- Has established visual literacy skills

- Takes an active role in recomposing visual and written information

- Is able to integrate cues from written and visual text

- Uses organizational formats for learning

- Has the opportunity to work in cooperative groups

- Has experience with compare and contrast questioning

Comprehension

- Has experience in the comprehension strategy of retelling

- Can recall, summarize and paraphrase what is listened to and viewed

- Has extended personal vocabulary

- Applies the skill of sequencing as an organizational strategy for comprehension

Written Experiences

- Has participated in a variety of age-appropriate writing experiences

- Uses prewriting strategies such as drawings, brainstorming and/or graphic organizers

- Is able to transfer ideas into sentences with appropriate support

Oral Language

- Is developing the ability to respond to what is seen and heard

Materials

- *A Little Duck Tale* video (see Ordering Information, page 152)

- index cards

- Story Event Cards from *Make Way for Ducklings* (page 103–105)

- drawing paper and crayons

- pencils

- notebook paper

- Fill-in Cards (pages 110–111)

- Word Web (page 113)

Before Class

1. Preview the video in order to understand where to stop the segment.

2. Copy the Fill-in Cards.

3. Copy the Word Web for class use.

Lesson Plan

1. Describe the plan for the rest of the unit. Remind the students that they are going to write a nonfiction book. The book will be based on a true story of a wild duck family living in Tokyo, Japan. They will gather information for the book by watching a video made during the actual events. In each lesson, students will watch a video segment of the live events and create a text version based on the events.

2. Show the first 10 minutes of *A Little Duck Tale*. Stop the video where Chibi gets out of the water for the first time. The narration will be above the children's complete understanding but this means they will rely more on the pictures and discussion to create their own descriptive text. This helps avoid simply copying the words from the video.

3. Mute the sound on the video and show the same segment a second time. This time have the children discuss what is happening by watching the pictures. Direct the discussion by asking questions to verify comprehension.

4. Lead a discussion to sequence the events from the story. Write each event on a separate index card and post. Students may choose to alter this list as they go through the rest of the activities.

5. Start a list of words to know and continue to add to this list as the lesson progresses. Include any words students request. Add words you think will be needed in writing the text. Brief explanations of meanings may prove helpful for some of the most unfamiliar words.

6. Give out the Fill-in Cards so that each group of two or three students has one. Do not give them out in the order in which they happened in the story. Read over the sentences. Have the children try to fill in the missing words. Show the video segment a third time (with both sound and picture this time) and have the students check their information. If some of the sentences are still not complete, have the whole class try

to fill in the correct words. Check for accuracy by reading all of the sentences aloud. If a sentence is incorrect go back to that part of the video and let all of the students try to fill in the information.

7. Have the students put the sentences under the appropriate event card. Review the events on the cards and change if needed.

8. Do a Word Web with the students to describe the setting of the story. See the example to the right.

9. Divide the students into groups and assign each group one event to illustrate. Have the students create the illustrations in pencil so the final book can be copied. When all of the pictures are assembled, have the students write the text that they think should go with each picture. Remind them that in the upcoming lessons they will write the text in their group. (If the students experience difficulty the activities can continue to be carried out as a whole group activity.)

10. Return to the Story Event Cards for *Make Way for Ducklings*. Where do the cards for this story match the ones from the book? (The Chibi video starts with the hatching of the eggs.)

Last year mother duck and her nine _____ crossed a busy street in Tokyo, _____.

Tokyo is the _____ of the country of Japan like Washington, D.C., is the capital of the _____ _____.

Again this year the mother duck appeared on the exact same _____. This year she hatched _____ ducklings.

People wondered if the mother duck would try to _____ _____ _____ this year with her ducklings.

These ducklings reminded people of the story of _____ _____ _____ _____ in Boston.

These ducks are called _____ ducks because they have a spot on their bills.

_____ people came to cover the story of the ducks living in a pond beside an office building.

Only _____ _____ after the ducklings hatched the Mother Duck tried to get them to come out of the pond.

The first time the Mother Duck tried to teach her ducklings to get out of the water it was 3:30 in the _____.

When the Mother Duck first tried to teach her ducklings to get out of the water one of the ducklings _____ _____ _____ _____.

The duck family tried to get out of the water _____ times the first day.

Every time the ducklings tried to get out of the water the first day one of the ducklings _____ _____ _____ _____.

The duckling that could not get out of the water was _____ than the other ducklings.

The people watching the ducks called the smallest duckling _____. They called him that because the word means _____.

On the second day of trying to teach the ducklings to get out of the water _____ _____ _____ _____ _____ _____.

Answers to Fill-in Cards

1. Last year mother duck and her nine **ducklings** crossed a busy street in Tokyo, **Japan**.

2. Tokyo is the **capital** of the country of Japan like Washington, D.C., is the capital of the **United States**.

3. Again this year the mother duck appeared on the exact same **day**. This year she hatched **twelve (a dozen)** ducklings.

4. People wondered if the mother duck would try to **cross the road** this year with her ducklings.

5. These ducklings reminded people of the story of **Make Way for Ducklings** in Boston.

6. These ducks are called **Spotbill** ducks because they have a spot on their bills.

7. **News** people came to cover the story of the ducks living in a pond beside an office building.

8. Only **four weeks** after the ducklings hatched the Mother Duck tried to get them to come out of the pond.

9. The first time the Mother Duck tried to teach her ducklings to get out of the water it was 3:30 in the **morning**.

10. When the Mother Duck first tried to teach her ducklings to get out of the water one of the ducklings **could not get out**.

11. The duck family tried to get out of the water **six** times the first day.

12. Every time the ducklings tried to get out of the water the first day one of the ducklings **could not get out**.

13. The duckling that could not get out of the water was **smaller** than the other ducklings.

14. The people watching the ducks called the smallest duckling **Chibi**. They called him that because the word means **runt**.

15. On the second day of trying to teach the ducklings to get out of the water **Chibi got out of the water**.

Word Web

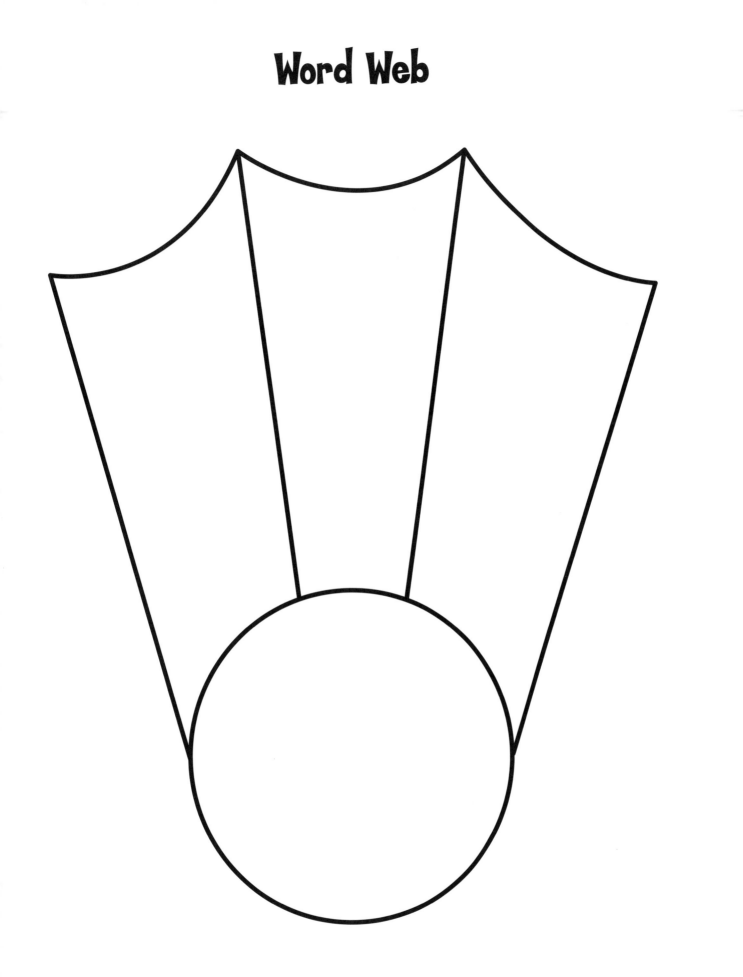

Duck Fever • Lesson 5

Lesson Learning Ideas

Techniques of Learning

- Has established visual literacy skills

- Takes an active role in recomposing visual and written information

- Is able to integrate cues from written and visual text

- Uses organizational formats for learning

- Has the opportunity to work in cooperative groups

- Has experience with compare and contrast questioning

Comprehension

- Has experience in the comprehension strategy of retelling

- Can recall, summarize and paraphrase what is listened to and viewed

- Has extended personal vocabulary

- Applies the skill of sequencing as an organizational strategy for comprehension

Writing Experiences

- Has participated in a variety of age-appropriate writing experiences

- Uses prewriting strategies such as drawings, brainstorming and/or graphic organizers

- Is able to transfer ideas into sentences with appropriate support

Oral Language

- Is developing the ability to respond to what is seen and heard

Materials

- *A Little Duck Tale* video (see Ordering Information, page 152)
- index cards
- drawing paper and crayons
- pencils
- notebook paper
- Fill-in Cards (pages 116–118)
- Word Web (page 113)

Before Class

1. Set the video for the second segment and preview it so you know where to stop this lesson's segment.

2. Copy the Fill-in Cards for student use. Copy the Word Web for class use.

Lesson Plan

1. Show the second segment of *A Little Duck Tale*. This seven-minute segment has the least amount of action of any of the others. Stop the video where the ducks try to go out the back entrance, decide against it and go back to the pond with the reporters following them.

2. Mute the sound on the video and show the same segment a second time. This time have the children discuss what is happening by watching the pictures. Direct the discussion by asking questions to verify comprehension.

3. Lead a discussion to sequence the events from the story. Write each event on a separate index card and post. Students may choose to alter this list as they go through the rest of the activities.

4. Start a list of words to know and continue to add to this list as the lesson progresses. Include any words students request. Add words you think will be needed. Brief explanations of meanings may prove helpful for some of the most unfamiliar words.

5. Give out the Fill-in Cards to every two or three students. Do not give them out in the order in which they happened in the story. Read over the sentences. Have the children try to fill in the missing words. Show the video segment a third time (with both sound and picture this time) and have the students check their information. If some of the sentences are still not complete, have the whole class try to fill in the correct words. Check for accuracy by reading the sentences aloud. If a sentence is incorrect go back to that part of the video and have the students try to fill in the information.

6. Have the students put the sentences under the appropriate event card. Review the events on the cards and change if needed.

7. Do a Word Web with the students about the news reporters.

8. Divide the students into groups and assign each group one event to illustrate. Have the students create the illustrations in pencil so the final book can be copied. Discuss the illustrations, then have the group create the text to go with it. If the students experience difficulty this activity can be carried out as a whole group activity.

9. Have each group share their picture and writing. Discuss how to make the text from the first day flow into today's text. If needed, go back to the book and share the transition words and phrases used to mark the passage of time.

Fill-in Cards

The Mother Duck led her ducklings toward the _____ at 6:15 one morning but the _____ frightened them and they came back to the pond.

Later the people decided that the ducks had not meant to go across the street but that they were just _____.

© 2005 by Karen A. Farmer Wanamaker (UpstartBooks)

The camera people got into an _____ about where people could stand to take pictures.

The rules for taking pictures became:

1. People with cameras had to stay at least _____ meters away from the ducks at all times.

TV crews watched the ducks for _____ and some even tried to _____ to get the ducks to _____ them.

The _____ had to be called in to help settle the disagreement of where to take pictures.

On the day that everyone thought the ducks would cross the road, it was windy and _____ so the ducklings hid under the office building's _____.

On the sixth attempt to cross the street the Mother Duck started out the _____ entrance. The news people followed but the sound of the _____ drove the ducklings and the reporters back.

Another rule about taking pictures became:

2. All cameras had to stay _____ _____ the ducks at all times.

Then one day the _____ duck flew onto the pond.

Answers to Fill-in Cards

1. The Mother Duck led her ducklings toward the **street** at 6:15 one morning but the **traffic** frightened them and they came back to the pond.

2. Later the people decided that the ducks had not meant to go across the street but that they were just **rehearsing**.

3. TV crews watched the ducks for **weeks** and some even tried to get the ducks to **talk** to them.

4. The camera people got into an **argument** about where people could stand to take pictures.

5. The **police** had to be called in to help settle the disagreement of where to take pictures.

6. The rules for taking pictures became:
   1. People with cameras had to stay at least **thirty** meters away from the ducks at all times.

7. Another rule about taking pictures became:
   2. All cameras had to stay **to the rear or side of** the ducks at all times.

8. On the day that everyone thought the ducks would cross the road, it was windy and **chilly** so the ducklings hid under the office building's **porch**.

9. Then one day the **father** duck flew onto the pond.

10. On the sixth attempt to cross the street the Mother Duck started out the **back** entrance. The news people followed but the sound of the **traffic (roar of civilization)** drove the ducklings and the reporters back.

Duck Fever • Lesson 6

Featured Video

A Little Duck Tale. Discovery Channel, 1985.

A true-life story that portrays ducklings in their struggle for survival in downtown Tokyo.

Lesson Learning Ideas

Techniques of Learning

- Has established visual literacy skills
- Takes an active role in recomposing visual and written information
- Is able to integrate cues from written and visual text
- Uses organizational formats for learning
- Has the opportunity to work in cooperative groups
- Has experience with compare and contrast questioning

Comprehension

- Has experience in the comprehension strategy of retelling
- Can recall, summarize and paraphrase what is listened to and viewed
- Has extended personal vocabulary
- Applies the skill of sequencing as an organizational strategy for comprehension

Writing Experiences

- Has participated in a variety of age-appropriate writing experiences
- Uses prewriting strategies such as drawings, brainstorming and/or graphic organizers
- Is able to transfer ideas into sentences with appropriate support

Oral Language

- Is developing the ability to respond to what is seen and heard

Materials

- *A Little Duck Tale* video (see Ordering Information, page 152)
- index cards

- drawing paper and crayons
- pencils
- notebook paper
- Fill-in Cards (page 122–125)

Before Class

1. Set the video for the third segment and preview it so you know where to stop.

2. Copy the Fill-in Cards for student use.

Lesson Plan

1. Show the third segment of *A Little Duck Tale*. This is not the end of the video but it is where this unit ends. Stop the video where the ducks get into the water around the Imperial Palace. The last line is when the policeman says, "Operation complete."

2. Mute the sound and show the segment again. Have the children discuss what is happening by watching the pictures. Ask questions to verify comprehension.

3. Lead a discussion to sequence the events from the story. Write each event on a separate index card and post. Students may choose to alter this list as they go through the rest of the activities.

4. Start a list of words and continue to add to this list as the lesson progresses. Include any words students request. Add words you think will be needed. Brief explanations of meanings may prove helpful for some of the most unfamiliar words.

5. Hand out the Fill-in Cards to every two or three students. Do not give them out in the order in which they happened in the story. Read over the sentences. Have the children try to fill in the missing words. Show the video segment a third time (with both sound and picture) and have the students check their information.
If some of the sentences are still not complete have the whole class try to fill in the correct words. Check for accuracy by reading the sentences aloud. If a sentence is incorrect go back to that part of the video and have the students try to fill in the information.

6. Have the students put the sentences under the appropriate event card. Review the events on the cards and change if needed.

7. Divide the students into groups and assign each group one event to illustrate. Have the students create the illustrations in pencil so the final book can be copied. After they have created and discussed their illustration, create the text to go with the illustration. If the students experience difficulty this activity can be carried out as a whole group activity.

8. Have each group share their picture and writing. Then brainstorm about the main idea of the story. This will aid in coming up with a book title in the next lesson.

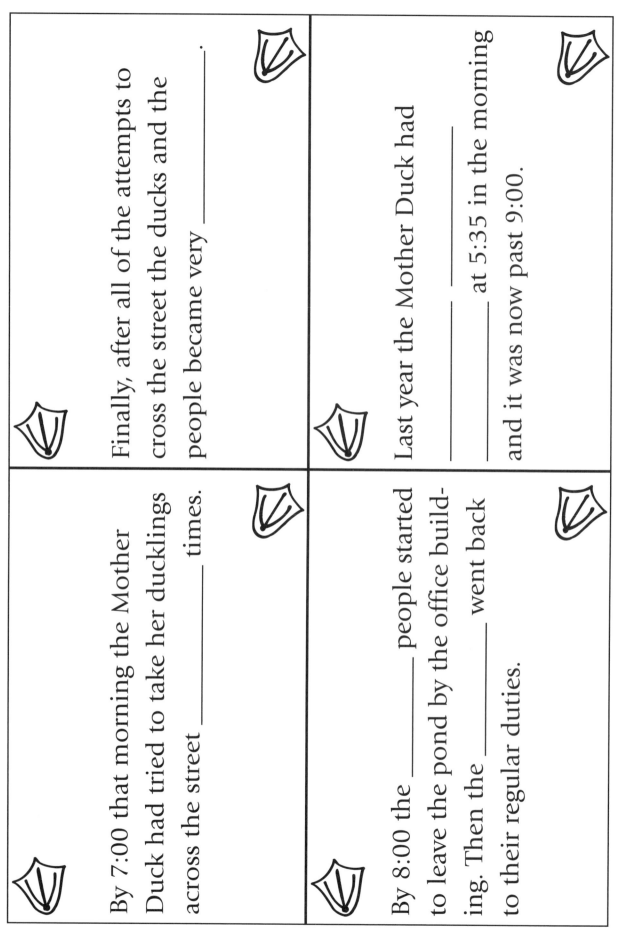

Finally, after all of the attempts to cross the street the ducks and the people became very _____.

By 7:00 that morning the Mother Duck had tried to take her ducklings _____ times. across the street _____

Last year the Mother Duck had _____ at 5:35 in the morning and it was now past 9:00.

By 8:00 the _____ people started to leave the pond by the office building. Then the _____ went back to their regular duties.

The ducks go _____ the _____, the point of no return. _____ This is because ducks cannot climb.

Who will help the ducks cross the streets? Finally, a _____ jumped out into the road to _____ _____.

Just when everything got quiet the Mother Duck led her ducklings _____ _____.

The traffic on the street at midmorning is _____ cars per minute.

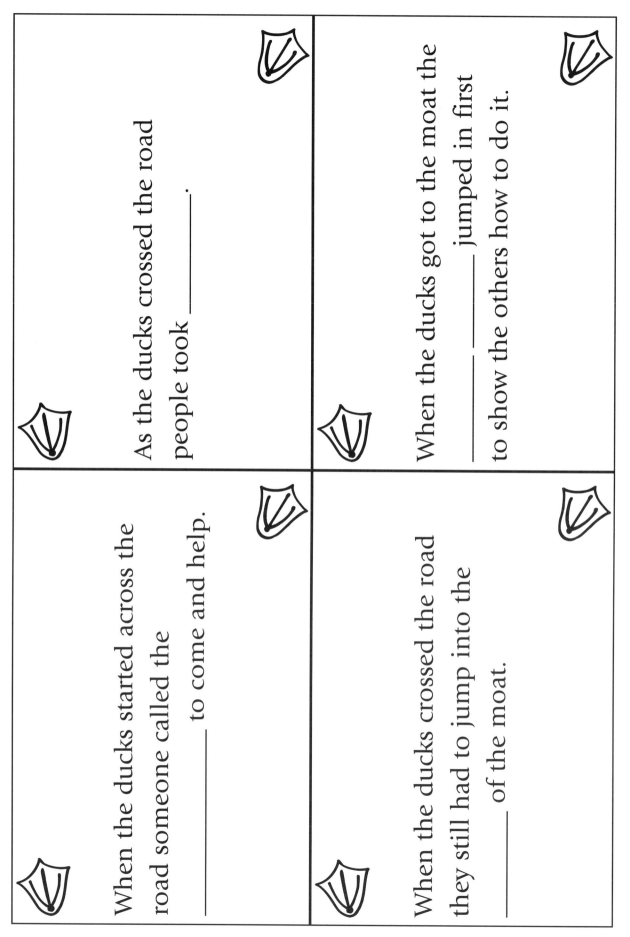

As the ducks crossed the road people took _____ .

When the ducks got to the moat the _____ jumped in first to show the others how to do it.

When the ducks started across the road someone called the _____ to come and help.

When the ducks crossed the road they still had to jump into the _____ of the moat.

_____ of the ducklings made it into the water of the moat around the Imperial Palace.

_____ was among the _____ to jump into the water of the moat.

After the ducks got into the water of the moat the _____ arrived.

Answers to Fill-in Cards

1. By 7:00 that morning the Mother Duck had tried to take her ducklings across the street **eleven** times.

2. Finally, after all of the attempts to cross the street the ducks and the people became very **tired (enthusiasm waning)**.

3. By 8:00 the **news** people started to leave the pond by the office building. Then the **police** went back to their regular duties.

4. Last year the Mother Duck had **crossed the road** at 5:35 in the morning and it was now past 9:00.

5. Just when everything got quiet the Mother Duck led her ducklings **out of the pond**.

6. The ducks go **down** the **steps,** the point of no return. This is because ducks cannot climb.

7. The traffic on the street at mid-morning is **300** cars per minute.

8. Who will help the ducks cross the street? Finally, a **crew member** jumped out into the road to **stop the traffic**.

9. When the ducks started across the road someone called the **police** to come and help.

10. As the ducks crossed the road people took **pictures**.

11. When the ducks crossed the road they still had to jump into the **water** of the moat.

12. When the ducks got to the moat the **mother duck** jumped in first to show the others how to do it.

13. **Chibi** was among the **last** to jump into the water of the moat.

14. **All** of the ducklings made it into the water of the moat around the Imperial Palace.

15. After the ducks got into the water of the moat the **police** arrived.

Duck Fever • Lesson 7

Featured Books

Chibi: A True Story from Japan by Barbara Brenner and Julie Takaya. Houghton Mifflin, 1996.

A true story of a family of ducks living in the Mitsui Office Park and Imperial Gardens in Japan, that had many people interested and watching them. ISBN 0395696232

John Philip Duck by Patricia Polacco. Penguin Putnam, 2004.

During the Depression, a young Memphis boy trains his pet duck to do tricks in the fountain of a grand hotel and ends up becoming the Duckmaster of the Peabody Hotel. ISBN 0399242627

Lesson Learning Ideas

Library Skills

- Is able to identify, utilize and create basic parts of a book

Literature Appreciation

- Has an understanding of how authors write books

- Has an understanding of the concept of artist and illustrator

Techniques of Learning

- Has experience with compare and contrast questioning

- Can appropriately access, evaluate and apply Internet-sourced information

Comprehension

- Utilizes the comprehension strategy of prediction

- Is beginning to comprehend basic text structures

Materials

- *John Philip Duck* by Patricia Polacco

- *John Philip Duck* video (see Ordering Information, page 152)

- *Make Way for Ducklings* by Robert McCloskey

- *Chibi: A True Story from Japan* by Barbara Brenner and Julie Takaya

- copies of the student-written book

- art paper and crayons

- Internet access

Before Class

1. If possible, make a copy of the student-written book for each student to keep.

2. Find and bookmark the Peabody Hotel Web site at *www.peabodymemphis.com/asp/home.asp.*

Lesson Plan

1. Show the cover of *Make Way for Ducklings* and ask the children to suggest why they think Robert McCloskey picked that title for his book. Look at the list of main ideas from the last lesson. Use them to help the children decide on a name for their book.

2. Explain that their book is just a draft like one that might be sent to a publisher. Remind the children how long Robert McCloskey said it took him to write *Make Way for Ducklings.*

3. Have each student create his or her own cover and title page to go with the book. Allow time for students to share their work. Give each child his or her own copy of the student-written book to keep or make several available in the free reading area.

4. Gather the class together and share the first chapter of *Chibi: A True Story from Japan.* Discuss comparisons of the student-written book and the published version. What do students like best about each book?

5. Tell the children they are going to experience another story about ducks that was based on actual events. Read the dedication in the front of *John Philip Duck* by Patricia Polacco. Explain about book dedications—what they are and why authors and illustrators include them.

6. Share the duck information from the Peabody Hotel Web site.

7. Watch the 15-minute *John Philip Duck* video.

Factual Fiction

Factual Fiction • Lesson 1

Featured Book

Goin' Someplace Special by Patricia McKissack. Simon & Schuster, 2000.

In segregated 1950s Nashville, a young African American girl braves a series of indignities and obstacles to get to one of the few integrated places in town—the public library. ISBN 0689818858

Lesson Learning Ideas

Literature Appreciation

- Has had experience with various literary genres

Techniques of Learning

- Has experience with compare and contrast questioning

- Uses organizational formats for learning

- Has experience in critical thinking questioning

Comprehension

- Utilizes the comprehension strategy of prediction

- Is able to make connections with prior knowledge and experience

Materials

- *John Philip Duck* by Patricia Polacco

- *Goin' Someplace Special* by Patricia McKissack

- T-chart (page 133)

- Twentieth Century Timeline (page 134) and Timeline Items (pages 148–149)

- dictionary

Before Class

1. Copy the T-chart for use with the class.

2. Create a class-size version of the timeline to use throughout the unit.

3. Visit the Kids Click! search engine at *sunsite.berkeley.edu/KidsClick!/.* Follow the "Picture Search Tools" link. At the next screen select "American Memory Collection." Then use any key word to search for copies of old photographs to print and use throughout this unit. These make excellent additions to the timeline and/or a bulletin board display. Students will need pictures to complete the book they will write in the fifth lesson.

Lesson Plan

1. Bring back the book used in the last lesson of Duck Fever—*John Philip Duck.* On one side of the T-chart have the students list the reasons why this book could be considered fiction and on the other side list why this book could be considered nonfiction. Remind students of the books they have studied that are considered science fiction. Ask what this book might be called if it was considered fiction. Explain that this book is considered fiction, but it is a special kind of fiction called historical fiction. Read the author's historical note in the back of the book. This is something often found in historical fiction books. Discuss what the word "historical" means.

2. Share that the students will investigate historical fiction based on the first half of the twentieth century. Ask the children what century they are living in. If the answer is not readily available pursue the answer by asking what year they were born. Use a dictionary to define the word "century." Explain that 2000 to 2999 is the twenty-first century. Ask the students what years would make up the twentieth century. Ask if anyone who lives today will be alive in the twenty-second century. Why or why not? Ask if anyone who lives today could have been alive in the nineteenth century. Why or why not?

3. Show the twentieth century timeline. Discuss timelines if the students are not familiar with them. Add some dates from your life that fit on the timeline. Tell the children that they will be adding information to the timeline throughout the coming unit. As each book is read, add the title of the book at the correct point on the timeline for when the story took place and add events from the Timeline Items on pages 148–149.

4. Show the cover of *Goin' Someplace Special.* Ask the children to turn to a partner and talk about where they think the girl in the story is going and/or where they would be going if they were going someplace special.

5. Read the book aloud. At the next to the last page of text, stop and ask the children to guess where 'Tricia Ann is going. What clues about the special place are given in the story? After some discussion, finish reading the story.

6. Share the author's note in the back of the book. Ask the students to place the story date on the timeline. This one is not as specific as the other books in the unit. **Note:** When I called the Nashville Public Library for a more specific date of integration, I was told that there is no more specific date recorded, but that it was sometime in the 1950s.

Why this book could be considered fiction	Why this book could be considered nonfiction

Twentieth Century Timeline

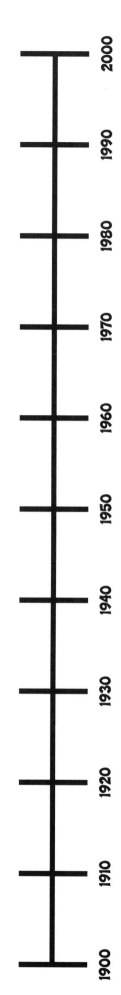

2000

1990

1980

1970

1960

1950

1940

1930

1920

1910

1900

Factual Fiction • Lesson 2

Featured Books

Hail to Mail by Samuel Marshak. Henry Holt & Company, 1990.

A certified letter follows its intended recipient all over the world as the postal service attempts to catch up with him. ISBN 0805011323

Mailing May by Michael Tunnell. Greenwillow Books, 1997.

In 1914, because her family cannot afford a train ticket to her grandmother's town, May gets mailed and rides the mail car on the train to see her grandmother. ISBN 0688128793

What Was It Like, Grandma? series by Ann Morris. Lerner Publishing, 2002.

Grandma Susan Remembers: A British-American Family Story
Grandma Esther Remembers: A Jewish-American Family Story
Grandma Francisca Remembers: A Hispanic-American Family Story
Grandma Lai Goon Remembers: A Chinese-American Family Story
Grandma Lois Remembers: An African-American Family Story
Grandma Maxine Remembers: A Native American Family Story

Lesson Learning Ideas

Library Skills

- Is able to identify, utilize and create basic parts of a book

Literature Appreciation

- Has had experience with various literary genres

- Has an initial understanding of the difference between fiction and nonfiction

Techniques of Learning

- Has the opportunity to work in cooperative groups

- Attends to personal and/or team tasks outside of the whole group setting

- Has established visual literacy skills

- Is able to integrate cues from written and visual text

- Has experience with compare and contrast questioning

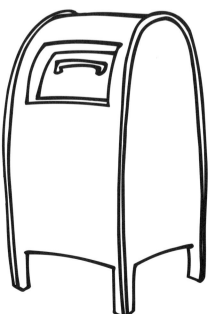

Comprehension

- Is beginning to comprehend basic text structures

Writing Experiences

- Participates in narrative writing experiences

Oral Language

- Is developing the ability to respond to what is seen and heard

Materials

- *Hail to Mail* by Samuel Marshak (see Ordering Information, page 152)

- *Hail to Mail* Reading Rainbow video, DVD or CD (see Ordering Information, page 152)

- *Mailing May* by Michael Tunnel (multiple copies if possible)

- What Was it Like, Grandma? series by Ann Morris

- My Postage Stamp visual (page 138)

- variety of postage stamps (see Ordering Information, page 152)

- drawing paper and crayons

- Twentieth Century Timeline (page 134) and Timeline Items (pages 148–149)

Before Class

1. Set the *Hail to Mail* Reading Rainbow video.

2. Create a transparency of the verso of the title page for *Hail to Mail*.

3. Gather and prepare materials for the group work as indicated in step 5 of the Lesson Plan.

Lesson Plan

1. Show the nine-minute portion of the Reading Rainbow program that shares *Hail to Mail*.

2. Explain that *Hail to Mail* is an illustrated poem. Show the verso of the title page on the overhead. Have the students locate information that proves this book is classified as a poem and not a rhyming book. Draw attention to the Dewey Decimal classification for this book. Allow the class to discuss poetry books as nonfiction.

3. Go back to the Reading Rainbow program and show the five-minute segment that covers following a letter. In this portion students see a present day example of a child writing to his grandmother and how the letter travels to her.

4. Introduce *Mailing May* by saying it takes place in 1914. This is also a story about mailing something to a child's grandmother. Read the book aloud to the whole class.

5. Divide the students into three or six groups depending on the number of materials available. Assign each group one of the following projects based on the Michael Tunnel book:

Group One: Use a copy of *Mailing May*. Locate and discuss the 12 photographs found as part of the illustrations in the book. Have the students pay special attention to four of the photographs—the pictures of the child, the child's house, the mail carrier and the grandmother's house. Instruct the class to create side-by-side pictures by drawing a modern day version of each photograph from the story.

Group Two: Return to the story to find out how much May weighed (48 pounds and 8 ounces) and how much postage it took to mail her in 1914 (53 cents). Using a United States Postal Service Ratefold from *www.usps.com,* find out how much it would cost to mail a package of the same weight today (use priority mail rates). Provide the students with a variety of postage stamps to view. Have the children share the information about stamp design from *www.stamponhistory.com.* Allow the students to design a postage stamp of their own using the My Postage Samp visual on page 138.

Group Three: Provide copies of *Mailing May* or the illustrations. Have the students participate in a visual scavenger hunt to locate as many things as possible from the illustrations that have changed. For example, lighting—in the book they show oil lamps and lanterns. Have the group create side-by-side pictures for each item found. Or have students search for the items listed in the box below. Each item is found in one or more pictures in the book. Have students mark the location of each item and check for accuracy.

Search Items

apple barrel	mail sack	scales
buggy	pitcher and bowl	steam engine
cash register	postage stamp	suspenders
coffee mill	postmistress	tin tiles
conductor	post office	train schedule
kerosene lamp	potbellied stove	trestle bridge
lantern	quilt	water tank

---

6. Read aloud the author's note in the back of the book and add the important dates to the class timeline along with events from the Timeline Items on pages 148–149.

7. Explain that the children have personal history sources right under their own noses. Share some or all of the books from the What Was it Like, Grandma? series. Tell the students that by talking to their parents, grandparents and other adults they can find out an enormous amount of information and stories about what it was like when they were young. Encourage the children to write a letter or talk to the adults in their family and/or neighborhood. As a class, create a general letter to a grandmother to explain what the class has been doing and some questions they would like to ask about life when their grandmother was a child.

My Postage Stamp

Factual Fiction • Lesson 3

Featured Book

Milly and the Macy's Parade by Shana Corey. Scholastic, 2002.

Concerned that the immigrant employees of New York City's Macy's department store are homesick at Christmas, a young girl inspires the store's head to hold the first Macy's Parade. Based on a true story; includes historical note. ISBN 0439297540

Lesson Learning Ideas

Techniques of Learning

- Has the opportunity to work in cooperative groups
- Understands and participates in brainstorming activities
- Can access, evaluate and apply Internet-sourced information

Comprehension

- Has experience in the comprehension strategy of retelling

Writing Experiences

- Has experience with examples of expository writing and its uses
- Participates in expository writing experiences

Materials

- Twentieth Century Timeline (page 134) and Timeline Items (pages 148–149)
- *Milly and the Macy's Parade* by Shana Corey
- Question Sheet (page 141)
- newspapers
- Internet access
- reference materials *(optional)*

Before Class

1. Locate Web sites featuring the Macy's Parade. Use any adult search engine and search on "Macy's Thanksgiving Day Parade" or use either of the following sites: *www.nyc tourist.com/macys_menu.htm* or *www.ny.com/holiday/thanksgiving/gallery.html*.

2. Make copies of the Question Sheet for student use.

Lesson Plan

1. In small groups, ask the students to create a list of words and phrases that they think of when they think about Thanksgiving.

2. Combine the lists into one and figure out the words found on the most group lists. More than likely the Macy's Parade of the Thanksgiving Day Parade will be among the top ideas.

3. Share with the children that today's story is a book about the first Macy's parade. Read aloud *Milly and the Macy's Parade*. After, ask small groups or pairs of students to complete the Question Sheet on page 141 based on the information from the book. Fill in the "Who" together to get the students started.

4. When the children have had time to complete the task, bring them back to a whole group setting. Show several newspapers to the children. Explain that what they have just done is what a news reporter tries to do when writing an article.

5. Combine the information from the student's Question Sheets into a class list. Use the class timeline to record the when of the story. Add events from the Timeline Items on pages 148–149.

6. Work together a a class to create a news story about the first Thanksgiving Day Parade. Remember to choose a headline and to include a byline. News stories usually start with the most important information first and work down to the least important.

7. Share some of the information about the early days of the parade from the Web sites. In addition, share the information in the author's note. Allow students to add some of this information to the article if they want to.

8. If time permits, have the students select one of the famous first facts from their timeline. Write a newspaper article about the event surrounding the fact. Use reference materials to find out more about the event. Then re-use the question sheet to outline the newspaper article content.

Question Sheet

Topic: First Thanksgiving Day Parade

Who: _____

What: _____

When: _____

Where: _____

Why: _____

_____

How: _____

_____

Factual Fiction • Lesson 4

Featured Books

The Babe & I **by David Adler. Harcourt, 1999.**

While helping his family make ends meet during the Depression by selling newspapers, a boy meets Babe Ruth. ISBN 0152013784

The Girl Who Struck Out Babe Ruth **by Jean Patrick.**
Lerner Publishing, 2000.

A retelling of the day Jackie Mitchell, a 17-year-old female professional baseball player, struck out the New York Yankees' best hitters, Babe Ruth and Lou Gehrig, in an exhibition game in 1931. ISBN 1575053977

Home Run: The Story of Babe Ruth **by Robert Burleigh. Harcourt, 2003.**

A poetic account of the legendary Babe Ruth as he prepares to make a home run. ISBN 0152045996

Lou Gehrig **by Richard Rambeck. The Child's World, Inc., 1994.**

A biography of the New York Yankee first baseman known as "The Iron Horse" because he played in 2,000 consecutive games. ISBN 1567660738

Lou Gehrig: The Luckiest Man **by David Adler. Harcourt, 1997.**

Traces the life of the Yankees' star ballplayer, focusing on his character and his struggle with the terminal disease amyotrophic lateral sclerosis. ISBN 0152005234

Mighty Jackie: The Strike-Out Queen **by Marissa Moss.**
Simon & Schuster, 2004.

In 1931, 17-year-old Jackie Mitchell pitches against Babe Ruth and Lou Gehrig in an exhibition game, becoming the first professional female pitcher in baseball history. ISBN 0689863292

Lesson Learning Ideas

Techniques of Learning

• Understands and participates in brainstorming activities

• Has the opportunity to work in cooperative groups

• Can transfer learning experiences across multiple situations

• Takes an active role in recomposing visual and written information

Comprehension

- Has the opportunity to participate in experiences that support the acquisition of fluency

- Utilizes the comprehension strategy of prediction

- Can recall, summarize and paraphrase what is listened to and viewed

- Is developing the ability to generate appropriate questions

- Has experience with reading for the purpose of extending knowledge and understanding

Writing Experiences

- Responds to literature in a variety of written formats

- Participates in expository writing experiences

Oral Language

- Is developing the ability to respond to what is seen and heard

Materials

- *The Babe & I* by David Adler (RL 2.8)

- *Home Run: The Story of Babe Ruth* by Robert Burleigh (RL 2.2)

- *Lou Gehrig: The Luckiest Man* by David Adler (RL 3.5)

- *Lou Gehrig* by Richard Rambeck (RL 3.4)

- *The Girl Who Struck Out Babe Ruth* by Jean Patrick (RL 2.8)

- *Mighty Jackie: The Strike-Out Queen* by Marissa Moss (RL 3.5)

- chart paper

- markers

- Twentieth Century Timeline (page 134) and Timeline Items (pages 148–149)

Before Class

1. Gather at least one book from the list above about each of the following baseball players: Babe Ruth, Lou Gehrig and Jackie Mitchell.

2. Prepare the books by covering the title and taping them shut.

3. Create read-along tapes for each book to be used if needed by student readers.

Lesson Plan

1. Present the books with the titles covered. Explain only the name of the person each book is about.

2. Divide students into teams and assign one book to each team. Within their groups have the students brainstorm what they know about the book and the person it is written about. (Students will probably know nothing about Jackie Mitchell, so encourage the group to predict making use of the picture on the cover and what they know about baseball.)

3. Allow each group to share the results of their discussion with the whole class. Provide an opportunity for the groups to read their book aloud or to listen to a read-along tape of the book.

4. Ask the student groups to go back to their brainstorming and add any information that they learned from the book they shared. Remind students to compile important dates to add to the class timeline.

5. Have the students mix about the room until "pair" is called. At that time they should find someone who did not read the book they read. Give students time to share and compare the books they read in their groups.

6. Introduce the concept of an interview to the whole class. Explain that in their original groups they will create questions that might be used in an interview with the person their book was about. Tell students about the tips for interviewers. Interviewers try to ask questions whose answers are not already known facts. Interviewers write their questions down in advance of meeting the person. Interviewers often use questions that begin with how, why and what. Interviewers use what they already know about a person to create questions. Have the whole class come up with some good questions and some not so good questions as practice.

7. Have the students return to their teams to create a list of interview questions. When time is called, ask the teams to select the two or three questions from their list they would most like to ask. Allow students to share their selected questions.

8. If time allows, add two more items to the class timeline from pages 148–149.

Factual Fiction • Lesson 5

Featured Books

At Home: Long Ago and Today by Lynnette Brent. Heinemann Library, 2003.

An introduction to how houses and their care have changed in the past 100 years, discussing materials used to build homes, various ways to heat and cool them and how chores have changed over time. ISBN 1403445311

At Play: Long Ago and Today by Lynnette Brent. Heinemann Library, 2003.

An introduction to how children's and adults' leisure activities have changed in the past 100 years, discussing how people play and relax at different times of the year, on special occasions and on vacation. ISBN 140344532X

At School: Long Ago and Today by Lynnette Brent. Heinemann Library, 2003.

An introduction to how education has changed in the past 100 years, discussing how buildings and classrooms, books and lessons, recess and after school activities and ways of getting to school are different. ISBN 1403445338

A Christmas Tree in the White House by Gary Hines. Henry Holt & Company, 2001.

President Theodore Roosevelt does not approve of cutting down living trees just to be used as Christmas decorations, but his two young sons try to sneak one into the White House anyway. ISBN 080506768X

Going Shopping: Long Ago and Today by Lynnette Brent. Heinemann Library, 2003.

An introduction to how shopping has changed in the past 100 years, discussing how the places we go to shop evolved from a general store to the Internet and how paying for items has changed. ISBN 1403445354

Lesson Learning Ideas

Literature Appreciation

- Has had experience with various literary genres
- Understands and applies nonfiction reading techniques

Techniques of Learning

- Has established visual literacy skills

- Can appropriately access, evaluate and apply Internet-sourced information

- Takes an active role in recomposing visual and written information

Comprehension

- Utilizes the comprehension strategy of prediction

- Is beginning to comprehend basic text structures

Materials

- Twentieth Century Timeline (page 134) and Timeline Items (pages 148–149)

- *At Home: Long Ago and Today* by Lynnette Brent (Times Change series)

- *At Play: Long Ago and Today* by Lynnette Brent (Times Change series)

- *At School: Long Ago and Today* by Lynnette Brent (Times Change series)

- *A Christmas Tree in the White House* by Gary Hines (Times Change series)

- *Going Shopping: Long Ago and Today* by Lynnette Brent (Times Change series)

- Internet access

- index cards

- *Famous First Facts* book or Internet version

- drawing paper and crayons

Before Class

1. Follow the instructions from page 132 to find and print copies of old photographs for this lesson.

2. Find and bookmark the Web site about White House Christmas Trees at *www.real christmastrees.org/whitehouse.html.*

Lesson Plan

1. Show the photograph of the Roosevelt family in the back of *A Christmas Tree in the White House* by Gary Hines. Ask the children to read the picture by coming up with information based on observing it. Examples might be that this is an old picture because people don't dress like the people seen in the photograph. Be sure to discuss why the students think this picture is in black and white. In the end, explain that this is a picture of Theodore Roosevelt, the twenty-sixth president of the United States and his family, that was taken sometime between 1900 and 1910.

2. Share the information on Christmas trees at the White House from the Web site listed above.

3. Read aloud *A Christmas Tree in the White House.*

4. Divide the students into small groups and give each group a book from the Times Change series. Give them time to look at the pictures. Ask the students to find the timeline in the back of their book. Have the groups decide which items from the book's timeline would fit on the class timeline. Have the students add these dates and information in the appropriate places on the class timeline using index cards.

5. Draw attention back to the Times Change series. Have students locate one place in their book that shows a picture from long ago on one side and one from the present day on the other side. Read and share the illustrations and text from each group.

6. Give students pictures printed from the American Memory Collection Web site based on topics covered in this unit. Instruct them to draw a picture that shows a similar activity or event from the present day. In addition, the groups should create brief text to go with each picture as was done in the Times Change series. If time allows have the students share their creations.

7. Introduce the reference book and/or Web site for Famous First Facts. Explain that this was the source of the timeline information throughout the unit. Select one or more events to research using the reference materials.

Timeline Items

1900–1910:

- first ice cream cone
- first coin bearing the likeness of a president
- first teddy bear
- first car to exceed the speed of a mile a minute
- first Father's Day
- first bubble gum
- first movie theater
- first hamburger
- first Mother's Day

1911–1920:

- first zipper
- first self-service grocery store
- first laundry detergent
- first toaster
- first white bread

1921–1930:

- first car radio
- first shopping mall
- first frozen food for sale
- first motel
- first national Christmas tree
- first Milky Way candy bar
- first Macy's Thanksgiving Day Parade
- first air conditioner for home use
- first cow flown in an airplane

1931–1940:

- first television
- first M&M candies
- first can opener

1941–1950:

- first hair dryer
- first disposable diapers
- first television commercial
- first microwave oven

1951–1960:

- first McDonald's restaurant
- first animated cartoon series on prime-time television
- first air-conditioned public elementary school
- first Holiday Inn hotel
- first sugar-free soft drinks
- first state admitted to the Union that did not border another state
- first Barbie doll

1961–1970:

- first Wal-Mart store
- first seat belts in cars
- first astronaut launched into space
- first cassette tape recorder
- first zip codes
- first astronaut to orbit the earth
- first telephone with push buttons
- first astronauts to land on the moon
- first Kwanzaa celebration
- first running shoes
- first aluminum cans with tab openings
- first computer game

1971–1980:

- first satellite dish for personal use
- first personal computer
- first pen with erasable ink
- first pressure-sensitive adhesive postage stamp
- first in-line roller skates
- first video game
- first videocassette recorder for home use

1981–1990:

- first Martin Luther King Day
- first compact disc players
- first female astronaut to fly in space

1991–2000:

- first movie that was entirely computer animated
- first chicken pox vaccine

Facts used with permission from *Famous First Facts* published by H. W. Wilson. For more information and exact dates use the book or online version.

Great Rip Roar Read Report

Pages torn

Pages missing

Written or colored in

Other

Name: _____

❀ Ordering Information ❀

Out of this World

Lesson 1

Alistair in Outer Space Video: Available from GPN.

GPN
P.O. Box 80669
Lincoln, NE 68501-0889
800-228-4630
gpn.unl.edu

Lesson 4

The Magic School Bus Gets Lost in Space Video: Available from many locations. One is the Library Video Company.

Library Video Company
P.O. Box 580
Wynnewood, PA 19096
800-843-3620
Fax 610-645-4040
www.LibraryVideo.com

The Magic School Bus Stamp: Available from Kidstamps.

Kidstamps
P.O. Box 18699
Cleveland Hts, OH 44118
800-727-5437
Fax 216-291-6887
www.kidstamps.com

Lesson 6

The Magic School Bus Lost in the Solar System CD: Available from Scholastic.

Scholastic
2931 E. McCarty Street
Jefferson City, MO 65101
800-724-6527
www.scholastic.com

Lesson 7

The Magic School Bus Lost in the Solar System Big Book: Available from Scholastic.

Scholastic
2931 E. McCarty Street
Jefferson City, MO 65101

800-724-6527
www.scholastic.com

Exploring Space Big Book: Available from National Geographic School Publishing.

National Geographic School Publishing
P.O. Box 10597
Des Moines, IA 50340-0597
800-368-2728
www.ngschoolpub.org

It's Raining Cats and Dogs

Lesson 2

Paws, Claws, Feathers and Fins Video: Available from Amazon.com.

Lesson 3

Should We Have Pets? A Persuasive Text: Available from Mondo Publishing.

Mondo Publishing
980 Avenue of the Americas
New York, NY 10018
888-88-MONDO
Fax 888-532-4492
www.mondopub.com

Lesson 4

Arthur's New Puppy Video: Available from Demco. Numerous Arthur related materials are also available.

Demco
P.O. Box 7488
Madison, WI 53707-7488
800-962-4463
www.demco.com

Lesson 6

Harry the Dirty Dog Listening Cassette or CD: Available from Weston Woods.

Weston Woods
143 Main Street
Norwalk, CT 06851
800-243-5020
Fax 203-845-0498
www.scholastic.com/westonwoods

Lesson 7

Officer Buckle and Gloria Video: Available from Weston Woods.

Weston Woods
143 Main Street
Norwalk, CT 06851
800-243-5020
Fax 203-845-0498
www.scholastic.com/westonwoods

Lesson 14

In the Wild Series: All of these books can be purchased in paperback from Heinemann Library.

Heinemann Library
6277 Sea Harbor Drive, 5th Floor
Orlando, FL 32887
888-363-4266
www.heinemannlibrary.com

Duck Fever

Lesson 1

Make Way for Ducklings Video: Available from Weston Woods.

Weston Woods
143 Main Street
Norwalk, CT 06851
800-243-5020
Fax 203-845-0498
www.scholastic.com/westonwoods

Lessons 4, 5 and 6

A Little Duck Tale Video: Available from the Discovery Channel Catalog and some Discovery Channel Stores.

Discovery Channel
Two Explore Lane
P.O. Box 788
Florence, KY 41022
800-627-9399
shopping.discovery.com

Lesson 7

John Philip Duck Video: Available from Spoken Arts.

Spoken Arts
195 South White Rock Road
Holmes, NY 12531
800-326-4090
Fax 845-878-9009
www.spokenartsmedia.com

Factual Fiction

Lesson 2

Hail to Mail Book and Video: Available from GPN. Book is only available from Reading Rainbow.

GPN
P.O. Box 80669
Lincoln, NE 68501-0669
800-228-4630
gpn.unl.edu

Postage Stamp Sets: Available in numerous locations such as Mystic Stamp Company. This company offers 100 historic U.S. postage stamps for $5, as well as free teacher materials.

Mystic Stamp Company
Dept. OC591
9700 Mill Street
Camden, NY 13316-6109
866-660-7417
www.mysticstamp.com